JOHN ANDREW BOYLE

GRAMMAR OF MODERN PERSIAN

PORTA LINGUARUM ORIENTALIUM
HERAUSGEGEBEN VON BERTOLD SPULER UND HANS WEHR

NEUE SERIE

IX

JOHN ANDREW BOYLE

Grammar of Modern Persian

1966
OTTO HARRASSOWITZ · WIESBADEN

GRAMMAR OF MODERN PERSIAN

BY

JOHN ANDREW BOYLE

1966

OTTO HARRASSOWITZ · WIESBADEN

Gesamtherstellung: J. J. Augustin, Glückstadt/Elbe
Printed in Germany

Contents

PREFACE

It is sometimes said that the Persians still speak the language of Firdausī and Saʿdī. This is true only in the sense that the English still speak the language of Shakespeare and the Bible: there have, in the course of the centuries, been very considerable changes in vocabulary, grammatical usage and pronunciation. In preparing a manual of the present-day language I have followed the same general principles as Salemann and Zhukovsky in their admirable *Persische Grammatik*, in which three generations of students have found the best introduction to Classical Persian. As in the older work a concise description of the grammar is followed by a chrestomathy with complete vocabulary: the main difference is the inclusion of a section on syntax. In the chrestomathy selections in simple Persian from school primers lead up to newspaper extracts and two stories from the well-known collection of folktales by Ṣobḥī. I have also drawn on Ṣobḥī for many of the grammatical examples. These are indicated by the letter S. Other examples (indicated by the letter D) are taken from the *Yād-dāšt-hā-ye safar-e Ferang* ("Notes on travel in Europe"), of Ḥ. B. Dehqānī-Taftī, now Anglican Bishop of Iran. This work, based as it is on the author's letters to friends, is written in a simple colloquial style and therefore lends itself admirably to use in illustrating the ordinary everyday language of contemporary Iran. For the contrary reason bellestristic writing, in which the influence of Classical Persian is still strong, has been deliberately excluded both from the grammatical examples and from the chrestomathy.

Apart from Salemann and Zhukovsky the works I have consulted with the greatest profit are those of Phillott, Lambton and, above all, Lazard, in whose *Grammaire du persan contemporain* we have for the first time a full and detailed description of the Persian language as it is spoken and written at the present day.

In conclusion, I should like to thank my friend Charles F. Beckingham, Professor of Islamic Studies in the University of London, for helping with the proof-reading and making a number of useful suggestions. I should like also to express my appreciation of the patience and courtesy shown by Messrs. Harrassowitz throughout the whole process of preparation and publication.

Manchester, March 1966 JOHN ANDREW BOYLE

Alphabet and Pronunciation

§ 1. Alphabet: The Persians make use of the Arabic alphabet, to the 28 letters of which they have added 4 new characters — پ *p*, چ *č*, ژ *ž* and گ *g* — to express sounds not represented in Classical Arabic. These 32 letters are written and read from right to left and, as will be seen from the following table, have for the most part different forms according as they are initial, medial or final, and connected or unconnected with the letters which precede or follow them.

Names	Unconnected	Final	Medial	Initial	Transcription	Examples			
alef	ا	ـا	ـا	ا	—	را	تا	کار	اسب
be	ب	ـب	ـبـ	بـ	*b*	باب	شب	کبر	بر
pe	پ	ـپ	ـپـ	پـ	*p*	پاپ	چپ	سپاه	پل
te	ت	ـت	ـتـ	تـ	*t*	توت	رست	چتر	تب
s̤e	ث	ـث	ـثـ	ثـ	*s̤*	حدوث	لجث	مثل	ثمر
ǰīm	ج	ـج	ـجـ	جـ	*ǰ*	تاج	کج	فجر	جنگ
čīm	چ	ـچ	ـچـ	چـ	*č*	پوچ	هیچ	بچه	چشم
ḥe	ح	ـح	ـحـ	حـ	*ḥ*	روح	ملح	سحر	حزب
xe	خ	ـخ	ـخـ	خـ	*x*	چرخ	میخ	شخص	خر
dāl	د	ـد	ـد	د	*d*	درد	تند	قدر	دل
ẕāl	ذ	ـذ	ـذ	ذ	*ẕ*	نفوذ	کاغذ	غذا	ذوق
re	ر	ـر	ـر	ر	*r*	دور	پیر	برم	راه
ze	ز	ـز	ـز	ز	*z*	باز	تیز	بزم	زن
že	ژ	ـژ	ـژ	ژ	*ž*	گاراژ	لژ	مژده	ژرف
sin	س	ـس	ـسـ	سـ	*s*	خروس	نفس	پسر	سیب
šin	ش	ـش	ـشـ	شـ	*š*	موش	ریش	بشر	شب
ṣād	ص	ـص	ـصـ	صـ	*ṣ*	حرص	تفحص	نصر	صد
ẓād	ض	ـض	ـضـ	ضـ	*ẓ*	فرض	تبعیض	حضرت	ضد
ṭā	ط	ـط	ـطـ	طـ	*ṭ*	شرط	ضبط	خطر	طلا
z̤ā	ظ	ـظ	ـظـ	ظـ	*z̤*	حظ	حفظ	نظر	ظلم

Names	Unconnected	Final	Medial	Initial	Transcription	Examples			
ʿeịn	ع	ـع	ـعـ	عـ	ʿ	موضوع	منع	شعر	عمر
γeịn	غ	ـغ	ـغـ	غـ	*γ*	باغ	تیغ	مغز	غار
fe	ف	ـف	ـفـ	فـ	*f*	بوف	حیف	نفر	فیل
qāf	ق	ـق	ـقـ	قـ	*q*	برق	حلق	فقیر	قند
kāf	ک	ـک	ـکـ	کـ	*k*	خاک	کیک	شکر	کس
gāf	گ	ـگ	ـگـ	گـ	*g*	برگ	ریگ	مگس	گرگ
lām	ل	ـل	ـلـ	لـ	*l*	مال	بیل	ملخ	لب
mīm	م	ـم	ـمـ	مـ	*m*	موم	سیم	نمک	میل
nūn	ن	ـن	ـنـ	نـ	*n*	قرن	دین	سنگ	نان
vāv	و	ـو	ـو	و	*v*	رو	سهو	مور	ورق
he	ه	ـه	ـهـ	هـ	*h*	ده	خانه	شهر	هزار
ye	ی	ـی	ـیـ	یـ	*y*	پری	نی	سیخ	یخ

Note 1: It will be observed that the alphabet, for the most part, falls into groups of two or more characters identical in shape but distinguished from one another by the presence, absence, number or position of the dots or diacritical points. It should be noted also that ن and ی differ from the group ب, ت, etc. only in the final and unconnected forms and that ف and ق likewise are identical in shape except in these forms.

Note 2: The letters ا, د, ذ, ر, ز, ژ, and و do not unite with the letter following. That letter, if medial, takes the initial, and if final, the unconnected form.

§ 2. Consonants: All these letters are consonants, though ا, و and ی may also be used to express vowel sounds. (See § 3 (b).) They are pronounced as follows:

ا —

As a consonant corresponds to the Greek soft breathing (') and is always used when a word in fact begins with a vowel. In this position it is ignored in the transliteration. Exx.:

اسب *asb* horse
اداره *edāre* administration
امور *omūr* affairs

ب *b*

As in English. Exx.:

آب *āb* water
شب *šab* night
سبز *sabz* green.

پ *p*

As in English. Exx.:

پدر *pedar* father
چپ *čap* left
پاپ *pāp* Pope.

ت *t*

As in French. Exx.:

توت *tūt* mulberry
دست *dast* hand
چتر *čatr* umbrella.

ث *s̱*

Occurs only in Arabic words. The original pronunciation was as *th* in *thing* but in Persian it is pronounced exactly as س *s*. Exx.:

ثروت *s̱arvat* wealth
بحث *baḥs̱* discussion
ثمر *s̱amar* fruit.

ج *ǰ*

As *j* in *jam*. Exx.:

تاج *tāǰ* crown
جنگ *ǰang* war
تجارت *teǰārat* trade.

چ *č*

As *ch* in *church*. Exx.:

چرخ *čarx* wheel
قارچ *qārč* mushroom
بچّه *baččе* child.

ح *ḥ*

Occurs only in words of Arabic origin. As ه *h* (see below) but pronounced in every position. Exx.:

حساب *ḥesāb* bill
حزب *ḥezb* party, sect
شرح *šarḥ* description.

خ *x*

As *ch* in the Scottish *loch*. Exx.:

خار *xār* thorn
شخص *šaxṣ* person
شاخ *šāx* branch, horn.

د *d*

As in French. Exx.:

دل *del* heart
درد *dard* pain
تند *tond* quick.

ذ *z̲*

Occurs chiefly in Arabic words. As ز *z* (see below). Exx.:

غذا *γez̲ā* food
کاغذ *kāγaz̲* paper, letter
نفوذ *nofūz̲* influence.

ر *r*

Always trilled. Exx.:

راه *rāh* road
دور *dūr* far
نرم *narm* soft.

Note: In the colloquial language final *r* is sometimes dropped. Exx.:

četoṷ < چطور *četoṷr* how?
bez̲ā < بگذار *begoz̲ār* let!

After *a* and *e* (both of which become as *e*) it is replaced by silent ه *h*. Exx.:

age < اگر *agar* if
mage < مگر *magar* except, *num*?
dīge < دیگر *dīgar* other
āxe < آخر *āxer* at last, after all
ūnqade < آنقدر *ānqadr* so (much)

The *r* of the particle را *rā* (§ 11 (a)), pronounced *ro*, is dropped after a consonant. Exx.:

ketābāro = کتابهارا *ketabhārā* the books

but

dastāšo = دستهایشرا *dasthāyašrā* his hands

ز *z*

As in English. Exx.:

مرز *marz* frontier
زن *zan* woman, wife
بزرگ *bozorg* great, large.

ژ *ž*

As *s* in *leisure* or French *j* in *jour*. Exx.:

ژاله *žāle* dew
مژده *možde* glad tidings
گاراژ *gārāž* garage.

س *s*

As hard English *s*. Exx.:

سیب *sīb* apple
سر *sar* head
پسر *pesar* son, boy.

ش *š*

As English *sh*. Exx.:

موش *mūš* mouse, rat
بشر *bašar* mankind
شراب *šarāb* wine.

ص *ṣ*

Occurs mainly in Arabic words. As س *s* (above). Exx.:

صلح *ṣolh* peace
حرص *ḥerṣ* greed
صد *ṣad* hundred.

ض *ẓ̌*

Only in Arabic words. As ز *z* (above). Exx.:

ضرر *ẓarar* harm, damage
حضور *ḥoẓūr* presence
فرض *farẓ* supposition.

ط *ṭ*

Mainly in Arabic words. As ت *t* (above). Exx.:

شرط *šarṭ* condition, stipulation
خطر *xaṭar* danger
طلا *ṭelā* gold.

ظ *ẓ̤*

Only in Arabic words. As ز *z* (above). Exx.:

ظرف *ẓ̤arf* dish, vessel
حفظ *ḥefẓ̤* preservation, protection
نظر *naẓ̤ar* look, view.

ع ʿ

Only in words of Arabic origin. Silent initially, it is pronounced medially and finally as a glottal stop. Exx.:

عمر *ʿomr* life
شعر *šeʿr* poetry
موضوع *moẓ̤ūʿ* subject.

غ *γ*

As the French *r grasseyée*. Exx.:

باغ *bāγ* garden, park
تیغ *tīγ* sword, razor
غار *γār* cave.

ف *f*

As in English. Exx.:

فیل *fīl* elephant
سفر *safar* travel
برف *barf* snow

ق *q*

Occurs chiefly in Arabic and Turkish words. As غ *γ* (above). Exx.:

قهوه *qahve* coffee
حلق *ḥalq* throat
برق *barq* lightning, electricity.

ک *k*

Palatalized in a final position and before *ā*, *e*, *i* and *ei̯*, otherwise as in English. Exx.:

کرم *kerm* worm
خاک *xāk* earth
شکر *šekar* sugar.

گ *g*

Palatalized under the same conditions as ک *k*, otherwise as in English. Exx.:

گرم *garm* warm, hot
مگس *magas* fly
مرگ *marg* death.

ل *l*

Finally softer than in English. E. g. فیل *fīl* "elephant" is pronounced as the French *fil* or the German *viel*, not as the English *feel*. Exx.:

لب *lab* lip
ملخ *malax* locust
سل *sell* tuberculosis.

م *m*

As in English. Exx.:

مادر *mādar* mother
نمک *namak* salt
سیم *sīm* wire.

ن *n*

As in English except before ب *b*, when it is pronounced as *m*. E.g. دنبال *donbāl* (*dombāl*) "trail". Exx.:

نان *nān* bread
دین *dīn* religion
سنگ *sang* stone.

و *v*

As in English, but silent in the combinations خوا and خوی, e.g. خواب *xvāb* "sleep", pronounced *xāb*, and خویش *xvīš* self, pronounced *xīš*. Exx.:

وزیر *vazīr* minister
جوان *ǰavān* young (man)
سهو *sahv* mistake.

ه *h*

As in English, but pronounced in all positions except, in most cases, when final after *e*. It is then omitted in the transliteration. Exx.:

شاه *šāh* king
شهر *šahr* town
خانه *xāne* house.

Note: In the colloquial language. *h* is dropped
(a) medially between vowels:

xām < خواهم *xvāham* I wish
šou̯var < شوهر *šou̯har* husband

(b) finally:

siā < سیاه *siyāh* black
eštebā < اشتباه *eštebāh* mistake
bārikallā < بارك الله *bāraka 'llāh* bravo!

(c) in the plural ending ها *hā* and the enclitic particle هم *ham* "also":

ūnā < آنها *ānhā* those, they
dassāto < دستهایترا *dasthāyatrā* thy hands
manam < منهم *man ham* I also
mām < ماهم *mā ham* we also

y

As in English. Exx.:

یاد *yād* memory
بیان *bayān* explanation
سعی *sa'y* endeavour.

Note 1. In the colloquial language, when a word ends in two consonants, of which the second is a dental, the dental is dropped in pronunciation. Exx.:

das < دست *dast* hand
nīs < نیست *nīst* is not
čan < چند *čand* several, how many?

Final *r* and *h* (2, *Notes* on ر *r* and ه *h*) are dropped under the same conditions.

Note 2: When a group of two consonants occurs medially between vowels and the first consonant is a sibilant, the second consonant tends, in the colloquial language, to be assimilated to the sibilant. Exx.:

(i) *ss* < *st*
feressādam < فرستادم *ferestādam* I sent
dassam < دستم *dastam* any hand
nīssam < نیستم *nīstam* I am not

(ii) *ss* < *sl*
messe < مثلِ *mesl-e* like

(iii) *šš* < *šm*
čaššā < چشمها *čašmhā* eyes

(iv) *zz* < *zd*
dozzīde < دزدیده *dozdīde* stolen

(v) *ss* < *sh* < *zh*
lāmassab < لامذهب *lā mazhab* accursed

§ **3.** The Short, Long and Diphthong Vowels (in the middle and at the end of words):

(a) The short vowels are not normally written. They can however be expressed by the use of the vowel signs, which are placed over or under the preceding consonant. These signs are:

(i) *fathe* (َ), represented in the transliteration by *a*:

بَد *bad* bad

دَر *dar* door

مَن *man* I

(ii) *zamme* (ُ), represented by *o*:

پُر *por* full

پُشت *pošt* back

ذُغال *zoγāl* coal

(iii) *kasre* (ِ), represented by *e* and *i*:

شِکَم *šekam* stomach

دِل *del* heart

سِیاه *siyāh* black

(b) The corresponding long vowels are expressed by the same signs (usually omitted in writting) followed by the consonants ا, و and ی. Exx.:

بَاد *bād* wind

کَار *kār* work

نَان *nān* bread

دُور *dūr* far

رُوز *rūz* day

چُوب *čūb* stick

شِیر *šīr* milk

مِیز *mīz* table

فِیل *fīl* elephant

Note 1: و sometimes represents the short vowel *o*. Exx.:

دو *do* two
تو *to* thou
خوردن *xordan* to eat.

Note 2: Final ى in Arabic words is equivalent to ـا *ā*. Exx.:

قرى *qorā* villages
عيسى *'īsā* Jesus
دعوى *da'vā* claim.

(c) The two short diphthongs, represented in the transliteration by *ou̯* and *ei̯* (sometimes *ai̯*), are expressed by *fatḥe* followed by و and ى respectively. Exx.:

دَولت *dou̯lat* state, government

مَوج *mou̯ǰ* wave

طَور *ṭou̯r* manner, way

مَيل *mei̯l* inclination

عَيب *'ei̯b* fault

شَيطان *šei̯ṭān* Satan.

(d) The long diphthongs, represented by *āi̯* and *ūi̯*, are expressed by ا and و followed by ى:

چَای *čāi̯* tea

پَای *pāi̯* foot

جَای *ǰāi̯* place

کُوی *kūi̯* lane

گُوی *gūi̯* ball

مُوی *mūi̯* hair

§ **4.** Vowels at the beginning of words: In this position they must be preceded by the consonant ا. See above, § 2. Exx.:

اَبر *abr* cloud

اُفُق *ofoq* horizon

اِسم *esm* name

اُوت *ūt* August

اِيران *īrān* Persia

آولاد *ou̯lād* children, sons

آيوان *ei̯vān* portico

اُوى *ūi̯* he

In the case of the vowel *ā* expressed by means of ا (§ 3(b)) the sign *madde* (˜) is placed over this ا instead of prefixing another ا. Exx.:

آب *āb* water
آهن *āhan* iron
آى *āi̯* come.

§ 5. Pronunciation of Vowels:

(a) Short Vowels.

اَ, َ, *a*. More or less as *a* in *cat*.

اَسب *asb* horse

سَگ *sag* dog

رَنگ *rang* colour, dye

اِ, ِ, *e*, *i*. As the *e* in *bell* except before *y*, when it is pronounced as the short *i* in the French *ville*. Exx.:

امروز *emrūz* to-day
ارتش *arteš* army
ميان *miyān* middle

Note 1: In the colloquial language *a* often becomes *e*, especially under the influence of *ī* in the following syllable. Exx.:

yek < يَک *yak* one
-eš < ش *-aš* his, etc. (§ 17)
kešīdan < کشيدن *kašīdan* to pull
refīq < رفيق *rafīq* friend, companion
nemīdūnam < نميدانم *namīdānam* I do not know

Note 2: The pronunciation as *i* is more general in the colloquial language. Exx.:

ātiš < آتش *āteš* fire
šiš < شش *šeš* six

Note 3: In normal speech the *e* in the verbal prefix *be-* (§ 35.3 and 4) becomes *o* under the influence of *o*, *ū*, or *ou̯* in the following syllable. Exx.:

bopors < بپرس *bepors* ask!
bogū < بگو *begū* say!
borou̯ < برو *berou̯* go!

اُ, ُ, *o*. As the French *o* in *pomme*. Exx.:
šotor camel
pošt back
toxm seed.

Note: In the colloquial language it sometimes has the sound of a short *u* as the French *ou* in *tout*. Exx.:
xanum < خانم *xānom* lady
angušt < انگشت *angošt* finger.

(b) Long Vowels.
آ, ـَا, *ā*. As *a* in *wash*. Exx.:

بَازَار *bāzār* market

فَارسی *fārsī* Persian (language)

پَاک *pāk* pure, clean.

Note: In the colloquial language *ā* becomes *ū* before *m* and *n*:
nūn < نان *nān* bread
būm < بام *bām* roof.

اُو, ـُو, *ū*. As *oo* in *roof*:

هُوش *hūš* intelligence

گُوش *gūš* ear

زُود *zūd* quick, early.

اِی, ـِی, *ī*, *i*. As *ee* in *feel* except in a closed syllable ending in *n*, when the pronunciation is shorter as in French *ville*. Exx.:

چِیز *čīz* thing

تِیر *tīr* arrow, shot

زمِین *zamin* earth

(c) Short Diphthongs.
اَو, ـَو, *ou̯*. As *ou* in *mould*,

نَوع *nou̯ʿ* kind, sort

رَوغن *rou̯γan* oil

فَوط *fou̯ṭ* death

اَی, ـَی, *ei̯*, *ai̯*. As *ei* in *reign*, except in the combination *ai̯y* followed by a vowel in which case it is pronounced as the English *ai* in *aisle*. Exx.:

صَید *ṣei̯d* hunting, the chase

حَیوان *ḥei̯vān* animal

صَیاره *ṣai̯yāre* planet.

(d) Long Diphthongs.

آی, ـای, *āi̯*. As *oy* in *boy*:

آذربایجان *āẕārbāi̯ǰān* Azerbaijan

نای *nāi̯* reed, flute

جای *ǰāi̯* place.

اُوی, نُوی, *ūi̯*. As *ui* in the German *pfui*! Exx.:

رُوی *rūi̯* face

بُوی *būi̯* smell

جُوی *ǰūi̯* stream.

Note: In the colloquial language the following contractions take place:

(a) *āya* and *āye* are contracted to *ā*. Exx.:

ād = آید *āyad* he comes
bās = بایست *bāyest* it was necessary

(b) *āyī* (*ā'ī*) is contracted to form the long diphthong *āi̯*. Exx.:

biyāi̯ = بیائی *biyā'i̯* (that) thou mayst come

(c) With the dropping of intervocalic *h* (see § 2, *Note* on ه) the following contractions take place:—

(i) *āha* (like *āya*) and *ahā* become *ā*. Exx.:

xād = خواهد *xvāhad* he wishes
čār = چهار *čahār* four

(ii) *āhī* (like *ā'ī*) becomes *āi*. Exx.:

xāi̯m = خواهیم *xvāhīm* we wish

(iii) *eha*, *ehe* and *ehī* become respectively *a*, *e* and *ī*. Exx.:

mīdam = میدهم *mīdeham* I give
bede = بدهد *bedehad* (that) he may give
mīdī = میدهی *mīdehī* thou givest

(d) *ava*, *ave* and *avī* contract to *a*, *e* and *ī* respectively in the present forms of رفتن *raftan* "to go" and شدن *šodan* "to become." Exx.:

mīše = میشود *mīšavad* he becomes
mīrī = میروی *mīravī* thou goest
bešam = بشوم *bešavam* (that) I may become

avān contracts to *ūn*, especially in the forms of توانستن *tavānestan* "to be able. Exx.:

mītūnam = میتوانم *mītavānam* I can
tūnes = توانست *tavānest* he was able

(e) *ūya*, *ūye* and *ūyī* contract to *a*, *e* and *ī* in the present forms of گفتن *goftan* "to say." Exx.:

begam = بگویم *begūyam* (that) I may say
mīge = میگوید *mīgūyad* he says
mīgī = میگوئی thou sayest!

§ 6. **Orthographical Signs**: Of these the vowel signs (*fatḥe*, *ẓamme* and *kasre*) and *madde* have already been mentioned. See above §§ 3 (a) and 4. The remaining signs are:

(a) همزه *hamze* (ء) representing the glottal stop. In the case of Arabic words it is written medially over ا, و and ى, which are simply carriers of the *hamze* and have no separate pronunciation, (ى in this position being undotted); and also finally after ا, و, and ى representing long vowels or diphthongs. In this latter position it is frequently omitted in Persian usage:

تأثیر *ta'ṣīr* impression
مؤمن *mo'men* believer
مسئله *mas'ale* question, problem
دواء *davā'* medicine
سؤ *sū'* evil
شیئ *šei̯'* thing.

In the case of Persian words it is used to indicate a hiatus between a long vowel and a following *i*:

پائیز *pā'īz* autumn
روئیدن *rū'īdan* to grow
زائیدن *zā'īdan* to give birth to.

It also has two other functions

(i) Placed over final silent ه *h* it represents the *eẓāfe* (pronounced in this case *ye*). See § 11 (6). Ex.

خانهٔ مرد *xāne-ye mard* the man's house.

(ii) Placed in the same position it likewise represents the glottal stop followed by *ī*, which may stand for the indefinite article (§ 9 (a)), the 2nd person sing. of the verb بودن to be (§ 41), or the ending ی -*ī* (§ 55 (h)). Exx.:

خانهٔ *xāne'ī* a house
دیدهٔ *dīde'ī* thou hast seen
قهوهٔ *qahve'ī* coffee-coloured, brown

It is also possible to write خانه ای *xāne-i*, etc.

(b) سکون *sokūn* (ْ) indicates that the consonant over which it is placed is not followed by a vowel. Exx.:

کرْم *kerm* worm
جنْگ *ǰang* war
گرْگ *gorg* wolf.

(c) تشدید *tašdīd* (ّ) indicates the doubling of a consonant in pronunciation:

ارّه	*arre* saw
بچّه	*bačče* child
محصّل	*mohaṣṣel* student

(d) تنوین *tanvin* occurs in three forms — ٌ *on*, ٍ *en* and ً *an* — representing respectively the nominative, genitive and accusative endings of the Arabic noun in its indefinite form. Only the accusative ending ً is common in Persian. It is normally followed by a silent ا but this is omitted if the word ends in ه (which is then written ة and pronounced *t*) or *hamze*.
Exx.:

کاملاً	*kāmelan* perfectly
شخصاً	*šaxṣan* personally
نسبةً	*nesbatan* comparatively
ابتداءً	*ebtedā'an* in the beginning

Note: It is common, though incorrect, to write, instead of نسبةً and the like, نسبتاً etc.

(e) وصله *vaṣle* (ٱ), placed over the ا of the Arabic definite article ال *al*, indicates the elision of the *a* after the final vowel of the preceding word. Exx.:

جدید ٱلورود	*ǰadīdo 'lvarūd* newly arrived (*lit.* new of the arrival)
مفقود ٱلاثر	*mafqūdo 'laṣar* lost without a trace (*lit.* lost as to the trace)
حتمی ٱلوقوع	*ḥatmīyo 'lvoqū'* inevitable (*lit.* certain as to the occurrence)

The *l* of the Arabic article is assimilated in pronunciation to the following ت *t*, ث *ṣ*, د *d*, ذ *ẕ*, ر *r*, ز *z*, س *s*, ش *š*, ص *ṣ*, ض *ẓ*, ط *ṭ*, ظ *ẓ*, and ن *n* and such assimilation is indicated by the placing of *tašdīd* over this following letter, the *l* being retained in the spelling. Exx.:

قوام ٱلسّلطنه	*qavāmo'ssalṭane* a title and name (*lit.* support of the kingdom)
حفظ ٱلصّحه	*hefẓo 'ṣṣeḥḥe* hygiene (*lit.* protection of the health)
مسقط الرّأس	*masqaṭo 'rra's* birthplace (*lit.* falling-place of the head).

Note: If the final vowel of the preceding word is long it is shortened in pronunciation:

فی ٱلفور	*fe 'lfour* immediately (*lit.* in the haste)
ابو الهول	*abo 'l-houl* Sphinx (*lit.* father of dread).

§ 7. Accent:

(a) The main stress normally falls on the last syllable of the word. Exx.:

پدر *pedár* father
خانه *xāné* house
شکسته *šekasté* broken
فردا *fardā́* to-morrow
مفصلاً *mofaṣṣalán* in detail.

(b) In the case of nouns this rule is modified insofar as the *eẓāfe* (§ 11 (6)), ی *-ī* as an indefinite (§ 9) and definite article (§§ 8 and 98), the particle را *rā* (§ 11 (a)) and the suffixed pronouns (§ 17) are enclitics and so have no independent accent. Exx.:

زنِ مرد *zán-e mard* the man's wife
زنی *zánī* a woman, wife
زنی که *zánī ke* the woman who
زن را *zán rā* the woman (*mulierem*)
زنش *zánaš* his wife.

(c) In the case of verbs

(i) The personal endings (§ 34) are un-accented.

دیدم *dī́dam* I saw
رفتید *ráftīd* you went

(ii) The prefixes می *mī* (§ 35, 1) and بِ *be* (§ 35, 3) and the negative نَ *na-*, *ne-* (§ 40) attract the accent to themselves:

می بینم *mī́ bīnam* I see
بِروید *béravīd* go!
نَرفت *náraft* he did not go
نمیرود *námīravad* he is not going

Note: The accent is irregular in ببخشید *bebáxšīd* pardon (me) and بفرمائید *befármā'īd* "please (come in, sit down etc."). Note also the colloquial *bérīm* (for *beravīm* برویم) "let us go," *berī́m* "shall we go?"

(d) Certain adverbs and conjunctions take the accent on the first syllable:

آری *ā́rī* yes
اگر *ágar* (or *agár*) if
اگرچه *ágarče* although
اما *ámma* but
اینک *ī́nak* lo! behold!
بلی *bálī* yes
حالا *ḥā́lā* now
مگر *mágar* except
ولی *válī* but

Note 1: هم *ham*, ام *em-* and دی *dī-* as the first part of a compound expression attract the accent to themselves:

همین *hámin* this very, the same
امروز *émrūz* to-day
دیشب *dī́šab* last night.

Note 2: چرا *čérā* "why?" and زیرا *zī́rā* "because" take the accent on the first syllable quite regularly since را is an enclitic. On the other hand note چرا *čerā́* "yes, of course," "certainly!"

Accidence

Articles

§ 8. Definite Article: There is no article in the strict sense. کتاب *ketāb* means "book" or "the book" according to the context: it can also mean "books" (§ 68). However the particle را *rā* (§§ 11 (a) and 64), which follows a definite noun in the accusative case, may be said to perform the function of the article:

آب بیار *āb biyār* bring water
آب را بیار *āb rā biyār* bring *the* water.

So too the relative suffix ی *-ī* added to the antecedent of a restrictive clause (§ 98) has the force of the definite article:

مردی که *mardī ke* the man who
کتابی که *ketābī ke* the book which.

Note: In the colloquial language the ending ه *-e* serves as a kind of definite article:

پسره *pesare* the son (in question)
دختره *doxtare* the daughter (in question).

§ 9. Indefinite Article: (a) This is expressed by means of the suffix ی *-ī* (not to be confused with the relative ی *-ī*):

کتابی *ketābī* a book
مردی *mardī* a man.

The hiatus between a preceding long vowel and this ی *-ī* is indicated by the use of *hamze* (§ 6 (a)(ii)):

پائی *pā'ī* a foot
موئی *mū'ī* a hair.

In the case of words ending in silent ه (§ 2) the hiatus may be expressed in the same way:

خانهٔی *xāne'ī* a house.

It is however usually indicated simply by placing *hamze* over the ه:

نامهٔ *nāme'ī* a letter.

In such cases the suffix may also be written separately from the noun (§ 6 (a)(ii)) and is always so written when coalescing with است *ast* "is":

بچّه ای *bačče ī* a child
دانه ایست *dāne īst* it is a grain.

(b) The indefinite article is also expressed, especially in the colloquial language, by means of the numeral یک *yak* "one":

یک ملت *yak mellat* a nation
یک کتاب *yak ketāb* a book.

یک *yak* may even be used in combination with the suffix ی *-ī*:
یک پادشاهی *yak pādšāhī* a king.

Note: The suffix ی *-ī* may also be added to plural nouns:
کتابهائی *ketābhā'ī* (some) books
مردهائی *mardhā'ī* (some) men.

Nouns

§ 10. Gender: There is no grammatical gender in Persian. Natural gender may be expressed

(a) by the use of different words:

مرد	*mard* man	زن *zan*	woman
پدر	*pedar* father	مادر	*mādar* mother
پسر	*pesar* son	دختر	*doxtar* daughter
برادر	*berādar* brother	خواهر	*xvāhar* sister.

(b) by means of the adjective نر *nar* "male" and ماده *māde* "female" (in the case of animals):

گاوِ نر	*gāv-e nar* bull	گاوِ ماده	*gāv-e māde* cow
شیرِ نر	*šīr-e nar* (male) lion	شیرِ ماده	*šīr-e māde* lioness.

(c) in the case of certain Arabic words by the use of the Arabic feminine ending ه *-e*:

رقاص	*raqqāṣ* dancer	رقاصه	*raqqāse* female dancer
ملک	*malek* king	ملکه	*maleke* queen.

§ 11. Declension: There are, strictly speaking, no inflections except the plural endings, on which see § 12. There are however various ways of expressing the cases:

(a) The accusative of a definite noun (see §§ 8 and 64) is followed by the particle را *ra,* which may be joined to the noun or written separately:

مرد را *mard rā* the man (*virum*)
زنرا *zanrā* the woman (*mulierem*).

Otherwise nominative and accusative are identical, مردی *mardī,* for example, being either "a man (*vir*)" or "a man (*virum*)" according to the context.

(b) The genitive case is expressed by means of the coupling of the two nouns concerned by means of the particle ـِ -e known as *kasre-ye eẓāfe*, "the *kasre* of annexation," or simply *eẓāfe*, on which see also § 14. By origin a relative pronoun the *eẓāfe* may be regarded in this function as equivalent to the English preposition "of". Exx.:

پسرِ مرد *pesar-e mard* the man's son (the son of the man)

دخترِ زن *doxtar-e zan* the woman's daughter (the daughter of the woman).

When the preceding word ends in silent ه the *eẓāfe* is indicated, exactly as the indefinite article ـی *-ī* (§ 9 (a)) by placing *hamze* over the ه. It is pronounced *ye* in this position as also after the long vowels, the pronounciation being indicated after ا and و (but not ی) by the insertion of ی *y*. ا is substituted for ـیٰ *-ā* (§ 3 (c) note 2) and ـی added as in the case of normal ا. Exx:

خانهٔ مرد *xāne-ye mard* the man's house

پایِ سگ *pā-ye sag* the dog's foot

بویِ گل *bū-ye gol* the scent of the flower

ماهیِ دریا *māhī-ye daryā* the fish of the sea

دعوای زن *daʿvā-ye zan* the woman's claim.

(c) Other relationships are expressed by means of prepositions, (§§ 45 and 46):

از مرد *az mard* from the man
بزن *bezan* to the woman
برای دختر *barā-ye doxtar* for the girl (daughter)
میان دریا *miyān-e daryā* in the middle of the sea
توی باغ *tū-ye bāγ* in the garden.

§ 12. **Number**: There are two plural endings: ـان *-ān* and ـها *-hā*.

(a) ـان *-ān*, the classical plural in the case of animate beings, is still commonly used in the written language. Exx.:

پدران *pedarān* fathers < پدر *pedar* father
مادران *mādarān* mothers < مادر *mādar* mother
مردان *mardān* men < مرد *mard* man
زنان *zanān* women < زن *zan* woman.

In the case of nouns ending in ـا *-ā* a euphonic *-y* is inserted:
آقایان *āqāyān* gentlemen < آقا *āqā* gentleman.

Final ـو *ū* becomes *-ov-* in pronunciation before the ending:
آهوان *āhovān* gazelles < آهو *āhū* gazelle.

Silent ه becomes *-g-*:
بندگان *bandegān* slaves < بنده *bande* slave
فرشتگان *fereštegān* angels < فرشته *ferešte* angel
نمایندگان *namāyandegān* representatives < نماینده *namāyande* representative.

Note: the plural in ان -*ān* may also be used in the case of certain parts of the body, mostly such as occur in pairs, and some other words:

ابروان *abrovān* eyebrows < ابرو *abrū* eyebrow
انگشتان *angoštān* fingers < انگشت *angošt* finger
بازوان *bāzovān* arms < بازو *bāzū* arm
چشمان *čašmān* eyes < چشم *čašm* eye
رخان *roxān* cheeks < رخ *rox* cheek
درختان *deraxtān* trees < درخت *deraxt* tree
ستارگان *setāregān* stars < ستاره *setāre* star
گناهان *gonāhān* sins < گناه *gonāh* sin.

(b) ها -*hā*, according to the classical usage, is the plural ending of inanimate objects:

شهرها *šahrhā* towns < شهر *šahr* town
روزها *rūzhā* days < روز *rūz* day
گلها *golha* flowers < گل *gol* flower.

In the modern language it is also normally used in the place of the classical ان -*an*, especially in the colloquial language:

مردها *mardhā* men < مرد *mard* man
زنها *zanhā* women < زن *zan* woman.

In the case of nouns ending in silent ه the ending is usually written separately:

نامه‌ها *nāme-hā* letters < نامه *nāme* letter
بچه‌ها *bačče-hā* children < بچه *bačče* child
خانه‌ها *xāne-hā* houses < خانه *xāne* house.

§ **13.** Arabic Plurals: Arabic nouns either take the Persian plural endings or else form their plurals according to the rules of Arabic grammar. Arabic plurals are of two kinds, "sound" plurals formed by adding an ending to the singular form and "broken" plurals formed by altering the vowel-pattern of the singular.

A. Sound Plurals: These are of two kinds, the masculine plural in ین -*in* and the feminine in ات -*āt*.

(a) The masculine plural is employed chiefly in the case of participial forms:

فاتحین *fāteḥin* conquerors < فاتح *fāteḥ* conqueror
محصلین *moḥasselin* students < محصل *moḥassel* student
مهندسین *mohandesin* engineers < مهندس *mohandes* engineer
مدعوین *mad'ovvin* guests < مدعو *mad'ovv* invited
مأمورین *ma'mūrin* officials < مأمور *ma'mūr* official
مخبرین *moxberin* reporters < مخبر *moxber* reporter.

Note: ین -*in* is the oblique ending. The nominative ending in ون -*ūn* is employed when the Arabic singular ends in ی -*ī* (-iy-). e.g.

سیاسیون *siyāsiyūn* politicians < سیاسی *siyāsī* political.

Note 2: The plural ending ین- *-in* should not be confused with the dual ending ین- *-ein*, which is also found in Persian:

دولتین *doulatein* the two states < دولت *doulat* state
مملکتین *mamlakatein* the two countries < مملکت *mamlakat* country
طرفین *tarafein* the two sides < طرف *taraf* side.

(b) The feminine plural in ات- *-āt*. This is added

(1) to nouns with the singular ending in ه- -e (in Persian also ت- *-at*):

درجات *darajāt* degrees < درجه *daraje* degree
آلات *ālāt* instruments < آلت *ālat* instrument
ساعات *sā'āt* hours < ساعت *sā'at* hour.

(ii) to verbal nouns:

احساسات *ehsāsāt* feelings < احساس *ehsās* feeling
امتحانات *emtehānāt* examinations < امتحان *emtehān* examination
اشکالات *eškālāt* difficulties < اشکال *eškāl* difficulty
تبریکات *tabrīkāt* congratulations < تبریک *tabrīk* congratulation.

(iii) to certain broken plurals to form a kind of double plural:

جواهرات *javāherāt* jewels < جواهر *javāher* jewel(s).

(iv) to passive participles used as nouns:

مخلوقات *maxlūqāt* creatures < مخلوق *maxlūq* created
موضوعات *mouzū'āt* subjects < موضوع *mouzū'* subject
مهملات *mohmalāt* nonsense < مهمل *mohmal* absurd.

(v) to certain masculine nouns:

حیوانات *heivānāt* animals < حیوان *heivān* animal
اثرات *asarāt* traces < اثر *asar* trace
نفرات *nafarāt* individuals < نفر *nafar* individual.

(vi) to certain Persian words:

دهات *dehāt* villages < ده *deh* village
باغات *bāγāt* gardens < باغ *bāγ* garden
کوهستانات *kūhestānāt* mountainous regions < کوهستان *kūhestān* mountainous region.

Note: A plural in جات- *-jāt* on the analogy of the Arabic plural in ات- *-āt* is formed from Persian and Arabic words in a- *-e* (ه), the ه being replaced by ج:

نوشتجات *neveštejāt* documents < نوشته *nevešte* written
میوجات *mīvejāt* fruits < میوه *mīve* fruit
سبزیجات *sabzījāt* vegetables < سبزی *sabzī* vegetable
کارخانجات *kārxānejāt* factories < کارخانه *kārxāne* factory
حوالجات *havālejāt* transfers < حواله *havāle* transfer.

B. Broken Plurals: The following are examples of the broken plurals most commonly used in Persian:

قلوب *qolūb* hearts < قلب *qalb* heart
اشخاص *ašxāṣ* persons < شخص *šaxṣ* person
ملل *melal* nations < ملت *mellat* nation
کتب *kotob* books < کتاب *ketāb* book
صنایع *ṣanāyeʿ* arts, industries < صنعت *ṣanʿat* art, industry
مساجد *masāǰed* mosques < مسجد *masǰed* mosque.
سکنه *sakane* inhabitants < ساکن *sāken* inhabitant
شعرا *šoʿarā* poets < شاعر *šāʿer* poet
قوانین *qavānin* laws < قانون *qānūn* law.

Adjectives

§ 14. The adjective is indeclinable whether used attributively or as a predicate. The attributive adjective usually follows the noun it qualifies and is joined to it by means of the *eẓāfe*. See § 11 (b). Exx.:

پسر تنبل *pesar-e tanbal* the lazy boy
پسرهای تنبل *pesarhā-ye tanbal* the lazy boys
پسرتنبل است *pesar tanbal ast* the boy is lazy
پسرها تنبل اند *pesarhā tanbal and* the boys are lazy.

Note 1: On the use of the feminine form of Arabic nouns see § 71.

Note 2: When used as substantives adjectives take the plural endings:

بزرگان *bozorgān* the great < بزرگ *bozorg* great
سفیدها *sefīdhā* white men < سفید *sefīd* white.

§ 15. Comparative and Superlative: These are formed by means of the endings ـتر *-tar* and ـترین *-tarin*:

بزرگتر *bozorgtar* greater
بزرگترین *bozorgtarin* greatest } < بزرگ *bozorg* great

تنبلتر *tanbaltar* lazier
تنبلترین *tanbaltarin* laziest } < تنبل *tanbal* lazy.

Note 1: The forms بیش *bīš* or بیشتر *bīštar* "more" and بیشترین *bīštarin* "most" serve as comparative and superlative to بسیار *besyār*, خیلی *xeịlī* and زیاد *ziyād* "many, much." So too به *beh* or بهتر *behtar* "better" and بهترین *behtarin* "best" are used as comparative and superlative of خوب *xūb* "good" alongside the regular خوبتر *xūbtar* and خوبترین *xūbtarin*.

Note 2. On the use of the comparative and superlative in Persian see §§ 72–4.

Pronouns

§ **16.** Personal Pronouns: The ordinary personal pronouns have the followings form:

من	*man* I	ما	*mā we*
تو	*to* thou	شما	*šomā* you
او	*ū* he, she	ایشان	*īšān* they.

Note 1: The accusative is formed in the same way as with nouns by the addition of the particle را *rā* (§ 11 (a)). Note however the forms مرا *marā* "me" instead of من را *man rā*; ترا *tora* (as well as تورا *torā*) "thee."

Note 2: The idea of possession may be expressed, as in the case of nouns, by means of the *eẓāfe* (§ 11 (b)):

پدرِ من *pedar-e man* my father (*lit:* father of me), *pater meus.*

پدرِ مرا *pedar-e marā* my father *patrem meum.*

However this idea is more commonly expressed, especially in the colloquial language, by means of the suffixed pronouns (§ 17).

Note 3: There are no possessive pronouns as such. The English "mine", "yours", etc. are expressed by the word مال *māl* "property" connected by means of the *eẓāfe* with the appropriate personal pronoun; alternatively the pronoun may depend on the preposition از *az* (§ 45) "from" or the phrase از آنِ *az ān-e* "from that (*i.e.* those) of." Exx.:

این باغ مالِ من است *in bāγ māl-e man ast* This garden is mine.

این اسب از شما است *in asb az šomā ast* This horse is yours.

آن کتاب از آنِ او است *ān ketāb az ān-e ū ast* That book is his.

Note 4: A purely literary equivalent of او *ū* "he," "she" is وی *veị*. او *ū* is in the modern language not generally used for "it," which is expressed by means of the demonstrative pronoun آن *ān* "that" (§ 20). So آنها *ānhā* "those" represents "they" when not referring to human beings and, in the colloquial language, entirely displaces ایشان *īšān*, except when used as a polite substitute for او *ū*. See § 63(b).

Note 5: In the colloquial language ما *mā* "we" and شما *šomā* "you" may take the plural ending and become ماها *māhā* and شماها *šomāhā*. This is because شما *šomā* like the English "you" is used to address a single person and ما *mā* is vulgarly often substituted for من *man* "I."

§ **17.** Suffixed Pronouns: On the use of this kind of personal pronoun, which serves both as a possessive and as an accusative or dative, see § 76. The forms of the suffixed pronouns are as follows:

ـم *-am*, ام *am* my, me
ـت *-at*, ات *at* thy, thee
ـش *-aš*, اش *aš* his, her, him, her, its, it
ـمان *-emān* our, us
ـتان *-etān* your, you
ـشان *-ešān* their, them.

Exx.:

پدرم *pedaram* my father
مادرت *mādarat* thy mother
برادرشان *barādarešān* their brother.

The separate forms (ام, ات and اش) are used in the case of words ending in silent ه:

خانه‌ام *xāne-am* my house
بچّه‌اش *bačče-aš* his child.

After a long vowel a euphonic *y* is inserted before the suffixed pronoun:

سرهایشان *sarhāyešān* their heads
پایم *pāyam* my foot
مویش *mūyaš* his hair.

Note 1: In the colloquial language the suffixed pronouns lose their initial vowel when joined to a word ending in a vowel:

پام *pām* my foot
برات *barāt* for thee
توش *tūš* in it.

Note 2: ـش *-aš*, unlike او *ū* (§ 16, note 3), is used for things as well as persons. In the case of things it is also used to express the 3rd person plural, ـشان *-šān* being normally reserved for persons.

§ 18. On the uses of خود *xod* "self" (and its purely literary synonyms خویش *xvīš* and خویشتن *xvīštan*) see § 77. In the classical and literary languages خود *xod* stands by itself in the sense of "myself," "thyself" etc. but in the modern language it is usual to add the suffixed pronouns:

خودم *xodam* myself
خودت *xodat* thyself
خودش *xodaš* himself, herself, itself
خودمان *xodemān* ourselves
خودتان *xodetān* yourself, yourselves
خودشان *xodešān* themselves.

§ 19. Reciprocal Pronouns: یکدیگر *yakdīgar*, همدیگر *hamdīgar* or *ham* express the English "each other" or "one another." هم, which is particularly common in the colloquial language, is used only after a preposition or the *eẕāfe*.

§ 20. Demonstrative Pronouns: The simple demonstratives are این *in* "this" and آن "that." They may be used either as adjectives or as pronouns. As adjectives they precede the noun they qualify and are invariable:

آن مرد *ān mard* that man
آن مردان *ān mardān* those men
این زن *in zan* this woman
این زنان *in zanān* these women.

As pronouns they take the ordinary plural endings:

ایناں *īnān*, اینها *inhā* these
آنان *ānān*, آنها *ānhā* those.

Note: On آنها *ānhā* as an equivalent of ایشان *īšān* "they" see § 16, note 3.

§ 21. From the simple demonstratives are derived the following compound demonstratives:

(1) with هم *ham* even, very:

همین *hamin* this very, the same
همان *hamān* that very, the same.

(2) with چن *čon* (a contraction of چون *čūn* "as," "like"):

چنین *čonin* as this, such
چنان *čonān* as that, such.

Note: The colloquial pronunciation is *čenīn, čenān.*

(3) with همچن *hamčon*:

همچنین *hamčonin* exactly as this
همچنان *hamčonān* exactly as that.

(4) with چند in the sense of "as much as," not "how much?" (§ 24 (6)):

چندین *čandin* so many, so much
چندان *čandān* so many, so much.

Note: چندین *čandin* also means "several."

§ 22. Interrogative Pronouns: These are:

(1) که *ke* who?

The colloquial form is کی *kī* and this occurs also in the plural (کیان *kiyān*, کیها *kīhā* what persons?) and in کیست *kist* "who is?," of which the second element is است *ast* "is" (§ 41.1).

Note: که *ke* "who," which may be followed by را *rā* and preceded by prepositions and the *eżāfe*, is not to be confused with که *ke* "that," the conjunction that also does service as a relative pronoun (§§ 50, 97 and 98).

(2) چه *če* what?

چه *če* is both pronoun and adjective. As a pronoun it takes the plural چها *čehā* "what things?" As an adjective it precedes the noun it qualifies which is often followed by the indefinite article (ی -*ī*):

چه کتابی *če ketābī* what book?

The colloquial pronunciation of چه *če* is چی *čī*, as in the first element of چیست *čist* "what is?"

Note: For چه *če* as a pronoun the colloquial language prefers چه چیز *če čīz* (*čī čī*) "what thing?"

(3) کدام *kodām* which?

is an adjective and precedes the noun it qualifies.

کدام شخص *kodām šaxṣ* which person?
کدام شهر *kodām šahr* which town?

Note: On کدام *kodām* as an indefinite pronoun see § 24 (3) and 4.

(4) چند *čand* how many? how much?

چند *čand* like the cardinal numbers (§ 78) is followed by a singular noun:

چند سال *čand sāl* how many years?

§ **23.** Relative: The *če* in هرچه *har če* 'whatever" (§ 24 (4)) and انچه *ānče* "that which," "what" may be regarded as a true relative. Here too may be mentioned the relative suffix ی *-ī* added to the antecedent of a restrictive clause (§§ 8 and 98). Otherwise the relative pronoun is expressed by means of the conjunction که *ke* "that" in combination with the appropriate personal pronoun, expressed or understood. See § 98.

§ **24.** Indefinite Pronouns: These are:

(1) کس *kas* someone.

کس *kas* is in the modern language regarded as a noun meaning "person" and serves as a pronoun only when followed by the indefinite article ی *-ī* (کسی *kasī* "someone") or in conjunction with other definite pronouns such as هیچ *hīč* "any," هر *har* "every," همه *hame* "all." For کس *kas* there may always be substituted the Arabic شخص *šaxṣ* "person."

(2) چیز *čīz* something.

Like کس *kas*, چیز *čīz* is in modern usage a substantive ("thing") and has the force of a pronoun only when followed by the indefinite article (چیزی *čīzī* "something") or when preceded by the pronouns هیچ *hīč*, هر *har* and همه *hame*.

(3) هیچ *hīč* any, anything.

هیچ *hīč*, which occurs only in negative or interrogative contexts, is either a pronoun or an adjective. An example of its pronominal use: هیچ نگفت *hīč nagoft* "he said nothing (lit. he did not say anything)."

As an adjective it precedes the noun it qualifies, which may be followed by the indefinite article ی *-ī*. Exx.:

هیچ کتاب *hīč ketāb*
هیچ کتابی *hīč ketābī* } any book.

With هیچ *hīč* are formed the following compound pronouns:

هیچ کس *hīč kas* any one
هیچ چیز *hīč čīz* anything
هیچ کدام *hīč kodām*
هیچ یک *hīč yak* } anyone (of several persons or things).

Note: On هیچ *hīč* as an adverb see § 47 (2).

(4) هر *har* every, each.

هر *har*, which is always an adjective, precedes the noun it qualifies, which may be followed by the indefinite article ی *-ī*:

هر کتاب *har ketāb*
هر کتابی *har ketābī* } every book.

It is used in forming the following compound pronouns:

هر کس *har kas* everybody
هر چیز *har čīz* everything
هر کدام *har kodām*
هر یک *har yak* } each (of several persons or things).
هر که *har ke* "whoever"
هر چه *har če* whatever.

(5) همه *hame* all, every.

As an adjective همه *hame* precedes the noun it qualifies and is more or less equivalent to هر *har*. Exx.:

همه روز *hame rūz* every day
همه کس *hame kas* everybody
همه چیز *hame čīz* everything.

As a pronoun it expresses the idea of totality and either stands alone or is joined by means of the *eẓāfe* to a following noun or pronoun:

همه رفتند *hame raftand* they all went
همهٔ مردم *hame-ye mardom* all the people
همهٔ شما *hame-ye šomā* all of you.

It is also followed by the suffixed pronouns (§ 17):

همه اش *hame-eš* (*hamaš*) all of it.

Note 1: In the literary language همه *hame* as a pronoun may take the plural همگنان *hamgenān*. This is however rare.

Note 2: A common equivalent of همه *hame* when connected by the *eẓāfe* with a following word is تمام *tamām* lit. "complete," "whole:"

تمامِ شهر *tamām-e šahr* all the town.

Other equivalents of همه *hame* as a pronoun, whether standing alone or connected by *eẓāfe* with a following word, are:

همگی *hamegī* totality
جمله *ǰomle* sum, total
کل *koll* all, the whole
کافّه *kāffe* total, whole.

Note 3: Here may also be mentioned the Arabic سایر *sāyer* "the rest," "remainder:"

سایرِ مردم *sāyer-e mardom* the rest of the people.

When referring to persons it takes the sound plural in ـین *-in*:

سایرین *sāyerin* the rest, the others.

(6) چند *čand* some, several

Like the interrogative چند *cand* (§ 22) it is followed, as an adjective, by a noun in the singular number:

چند کتاب *čand ketāb* several books.

As a pronoun it is found only in چندی *čandī* or یک چندی *yek čandī* "some time."

Note: بعضی *ba'ẓī* and برخی *barxī* "some," "certain," which formally are nouns followed by the indefinite article, function both as adjectives and as pronouns:

بعضی اوقات *ba'ẓī ouqāt* sometimes

برخی زنان *barxī zanān* some women

بعضی میگویند *ba'ẓī mīgūyand* some say.

(7) یک *yak* one.

The cardinal number یک *yak* (§ 25), when followed by the indefinite article, is employed as an indefinite pronoun:

یکی از آنها *yakī az ānhā* one of them.

It also occurs in combination with other indefinite pronouns. See above, § 19 and (§ 24 (3) and (4)).

(8) کدام *kodām* one.

On کدام *kodām* as an interrogative pronoun see § 22 (3). As an indefinite pronoun it occurs only in combination with هیچ *hīč* and هر *har*. See above, (§ 24 (3) and (4)).

(9) دیگر *dīgar* other.

As an adjective it follows the noun it qualifies and is joined to it in the normal way by means of *eẓāfe*.

مرد دیگر *mard-e dīgar* the other man.

As a pronoun it takes the indefinite article and the plural endings in ـان *-ān* and ـها *-hā*:

دیگری *dīgarī* another

دیگران *dīgarān* } others.
دیگرها *dīgarhā* }

Note 1: دیگر *dīgar* combines with یکر *yak* and هم *ham* to form the reciprocal pronoun. See § 19.

Note 2: On دیگر *dīgar* as an adverb see § 47 (2).

(10) فلان *folān* such-and-such, so-and-so.

As an adjective فلان *folān* precedes the noun it qualifies:

فلان کتاب *folān ketāb* such-and-such a book

As a pronoun it is usually followed by the indefinite article:

فلانی *folānī* so-and-so.

Numerals

§ 25. Cardinals: The cardinal numbers have the following forms

1	(١)	یک	*yak*	11	(١١)	یازده	*yāzdah*
2	(٢)	دو	*do*	12	(١٢)	دوازده	*davāzdah*
3	(٣)	سه	*se*	13	(١٣)	سیزده	*sīzdah*
4	(٤)	چهار	*čahār*	14	(١٤)	چهارده	*čahārdah*
5	(٥)	پنج	*panǰ*	15	(١٥)	پانزده	*pānzdah*
6	(٦)	شش	*šeš*	16	(١٦)	شانزده	*šānzdah*
7	(٧)	هفت	*haft*	17	(١٧)	هفده	*hefdah*
8	(٨)	هشت	*hašt*	18	(١٨)	هژده	*hezdah*
9	(٩)	نه	*noh*	19	(١٩)	نوزده	*nūzdah*
10	(١٠)	ده	*dah*	20	(٢٠)	بیست	*bīst.*

The remaining tens and the hundreds etc. are expressed as follows:

30	(٣٠)	سی	*sī*	400	(٤٠٠)	چهارصد	*čahār ṣad*
40	(٤٠)	چهل	*čehel*	500	(٥٠٠)	پانصد	*pānṣad*
50	(٥٠)	پنجاه	*panǰāh*	600	(٦٠٠)	شش صد	*šeš ṣad*
60	(٦٠)	شصت	*šaṣt*	700	(٧٠٠)	هفت صد	*haft ṣad*
70	(٧٠)	هفتاد	*haftād*	800	(٨٠٠)	هشت صد	*hašt ṣad*
80	(٨٠)	هشتاد	*haštād*	900	(٩٠٠)	نه صد	*noh ṣad*
90	(٩٠)	نود	*navad*	1000	(١٠٠٠)	هزار	*hazār*
100	(١٠٠)	صد	*ṣad*	2000	(٢٠٠٠)	دو هزار	*do hazār*
200	(٢٠٠)	دویست	*devīst*	3000	(٣٠٠٠)	سه هزار	*se hazār*
300	(٣٠٠)	سیصد	*sīṣad*	1000000	(١٠٠٠٠٠٠)	ملیون	*meliyūn.*

Compound numerals follow the same order as in English, i.e. the larger numbers come first, and they are linked together by the conjunction و *o* "and" (§ 50). Exx.:

پنجاه و هشت *panǰāh o hašt* 58
صد و پنجاه و هشت *ṣad o panǰāh o hašt* 158.
هزار و نه صد و پنجاه و هشت *hazār o noh ṣad o panǰāh o hašt* 1958

Note 1: صد *ṣad* and هزار *hazār* may take the plural endings ـان *-ān* and ـها *-hā* when standing alone or in apposition to a following noun:

صدها کتاب *ṣadhā ketāb* hundreds of books
هزاران سال *hazārān sāl* thousands of years.

Note 2: On the syntax of the cardinal numbers see § 78.

§ 26. Ordinals: The ordinal numerals are formed from the cardinals by means of the suffix ـُم *-om*, which in the case of a compound number is added to the final component. Exx.:

چهارم *čahārom* 4th < چهار *čahār* 4
دهم *dahom* 10th < ده *dah* 10
بیست و پنجم *bīst o panǰom* 25th < بیست و پنج *bīst o panǰ* 25.

The following are slightly irregular:

دوّم *dovvom* 2nd *do* 2
سوّم *sevvom* 3rd *se* 3.

Alternative forms are دویم *doịyom* and سیوم *seịyom.*
The regular یکم *yakom* "first" occurs normally only as the final element of a compound numeral. Exx.:

بیست و یکم *bīst o yakom* 21st
پنجاه و یکم *panǰāh o yakom* 51st.

Otherwise the equivalent Arabic ordinal اوّل *avval* is generally substituted

کتاب اول *ketāb-e avval* the first book.

The archaic نخست *noxost* has been revived and occurs in such expressions as نخست وزیر *noxost vazīr* "prime minister."

Besides the ordinals in ـُم *-om,* which follow the noun they qualify and are connected, with it by the *eẕāfe,* there are also ordinals in ـُمین *-omin,* i.e. ـُم *-om* plus an additional suffix ـین *-in,* which precede the noun:

صدمین سال *ṣadomin sāl* the 100th year.

Note 1: The ending ـین *-in* is also added to اول *avval* and نخست *noxost* "first" and آخر *āxer* "last" yielding the forms اولین *avvalin,* نخستین *noxostin* and آخرین *āxerin.*

Note 2: For the smaller numbers the corresponding Arabic ordinals are sometimes substituted in the literary language, as is normal in the case of اول *avval* "first":

ثانی *s̱ānī* 2nd
ثالث *s̱āles̱* 3rd
رابع *rābe'* 4th
خامس *xāmes* 5th.

Note 3: The ordinals in ـُم *-om,* like the corresponding Arabic ordinals in the accusative case (see above, note 2), may also be used as adverbial numerals:

چهارم *čahārom* fourthly
نهم *nohom* ninthly
ثانیاً *s̱āniyan* secondly
خامساً *xāmesan* fifthly.

§ 27. Distributives are formed by repetition of the cardinal numbers:

دو دو *do do* two by two.

yak "one" takes the ending ـی *-ī* (§ 9) when so used:

یکی یکی *yakī yakī* one by one.

§ 28. Multiplicatives are formed from the cardinals by means of the ending ـگانه *-gāne* (§ 55 (b) note 1) or by conjunction with the word لا *lā* "fold." Exx.:

دوگانه *dogāne* } double
دولا *dolā* }
سه گانه *se gāne* triple.

§ 29. The adverbial multiplicatives are expressed by means of the cardinals followed by بار *bār*, دفعه *daf'e* or مرتبه *martabe* "time" ("*fois*"):

دو بار *do bār* twice
سه دفعه *se daf'e* three times
چهار مرتبه *čahār martabe* four times.

§ 30. Fractions: The Arabic terms are most frequently employed. Exx.:

نصف *neṣf* half
ثلث *s̱ols̱* third
خمس *xoms.* fifth.

The Persian نیم *nīm* is also used for "half." It precedes the noun without the *eẕāfe*:

نیم ساعت *nīm sā'at* half an hour

The literary variant نیمه *nīme* takes the *eẕāfe*:

نیمهٔ روز *nīme-ye rūz* half the day.

Otherwise fractions are expressed by means of two cardinals in apposition, the denominator preceding the numerator. Exx.:

سه یک *se yak* $\frac{1}{3}$
چهار یک *čahār yak* $\frac{1}{4}$
شش یک *šeš yak* $\frac{1}{6}$

Fractions with large denominators are expressed in the same way as in English: یک شصت و چهارم *yak šaṣt o čahārom* one sixty-fourth.

Verbs

§ 31. The structure of the Persian verb is regular in the extreme. All the simple tenses are formed from one of two stems, the present and the past, and the personal endings are in either case identical except that the second person singular of the Imperative and the third person singular of the Past Definite and Imperfect (§ 36, 1 and 2) have no termination, consisting of the bare stem. On the personal endings see § 34.

§ 32. Verbal Stems: The past stem is in all classes of verbs obtained simply by striking off the final ـن *-an* of the infinative in ـدن *-dan* or ـتن *-tan*. Thus the past stem of پرسیدن *porsīdan* to ask is پرسید *porsīd*, that of رفتن *raftan* to go رفت *raft*.

§ 33. The rules for obtaining the present stem vary according to the class of verbs:

I. Verbs in ـیدن *-īdan*

These are by far the commonest type of verbs, there being a tendency to increase their numbers by adding ـیدن *-īdan* to the present stem of other classes, e.g. زائیدن *zā'īdan* < زادن *zādan* (II), روئیدن *rū'īdan* < رستن *rostan* (VIII (c)), کوبیدن *kūbīdan* < کوفتن *kūftan* (X). The present stem is obtained by striking off the ending. Exx.:

	Infinitive		Present Stem	
رسیدن	*rasīdan*	to arrive	رس	*ras*
بریدن	*borīdan*	to cut	بر	*bor*
گزیدن	*gazīdan*	to bite	گز	*gaz*
دریدن	*darīdan*	to tear	در	*dar.*

The following verbs in ـیدن *-īdan* may, for practical purposes, be regarded as exceptions to this rule, though the *-ī-* is in fact part of the stem:

	Infinitive		Present Stem	
افریدن	*āferīdan*	to create	آفرین	*āferin*
چیدن	*čīdan*	to pluck	چین	*čīn-*, *čin*
دیدن	*dīdan*	to see	بین	*bin*
شنیدن	*šenīdan*	to hear	شنو	*šenav-*, *šenou̯*
گزیدن	*gozīdan*	to choose	گزین	*gozīn.*

II. Verbs in ـادن *-ādan*

These likewise reject the ending.

	Infinitive		Present Stem	
افتادن	*oftādan*	to fall	افت	*oft*
ایستادن	*īstādan*	to stand	ایست	*īst*
فرستادن	*ferestādan*	to send	فرست	*ferest*
نهادن	*nehādan*	to place	نه	*neh.*

In the following exceptions to this rule the *-ā-* is not part of the ending:

	Infinitive		Present Stem	
دادن	*dādan*	to give	ده	*deh*
زادن	*zādan*	to give birth to, to bear	زا	*zā*
ستادن	*setādan*	to take, sieze	ستان	*setān.*

III. Verbs in ـودن *-ūdan*

These reject the termination and substitute ـا *-ā.*

	Infinitive		Present Stem	
آزمودن	*āzmūdan*	to test	آزما	*āzmā*
آلودن	*ālūdan*	to pollute	آلا	*ālā*
افزودن	*afzūdan*	to increase	افزا	*afzā*

	Infinitive		Present Stem	
اندودن	*andūdan*	to swear	اندا	*andā*
بخشودن	*baxšūdan*	to forgive	بخشا	*baxšā*
پالودن	*pālūdan*	to filter	پالا	*pālā*
پیمودن	*peịmūdan*	to measure	پیما	*peịmā*
ربودن	*robūdan*	to rob	ربا	*robā*
زدودن	*zadūdan*	to scour	زدا	*zadā*
ستودن	*sotūdan*	to praise	ستا	*setā*
سرودن	*sorūdan*	to sing	سرا	*sarā*
سودن	*sūdan*	to rub	سا	*sā*
فرمودن	*farmūdan*	to command	فرما	*farmā*
گشودن	*gošūdan*	to open	گشا	*gošā*
نمودن	*namūdan*	to show	نما	*namā.*

Exceptions:

	Infinitive		Present Stem	
بودن	*būdan*	to be	باش	*bāš*
درودن	*dorūdan*	to reap	درو	*dorav-, dorou̯*
غنودن	*γonūdan*	to sleep	غنو	*γonav-, γonou̯.*

IV. Verbs in ـردن *-rdan*

The following reject the ending ـدن *-dan* for the root, with or without alteration of the vowel:

	Infinitive		Present Stem	
آوردن	*āvordan*	to bring	آور	*āvar*
بردن	*bordan*	to take	بر	*bar*
پروردن	*parvardan*	to rear	پرور	*parvar*
خوردن	*xordan*	to eat	خور	*xor*
گزاردن	*gozārdan*	to execute, carry out	گزار	*gozār.*

The following lengthen the vowel:

	Infinitive		Present Stem	
آزردن	*āzordan*	to annoy	آزار	*āzār*
افشردن	*afšordan*	to press, squeeze	افشار	*afšār*
فشردن	*fešordan*	to press, squeeze	فشار	*fešār*
سپردن	*separdan*	to entrust	سپار	*sepār*
شمردن	*šomordan*	to count	شمار	*šomār.*

The following are quite irregular:

	Infinitive		Present Stem	
کردن	*kardan*	to make, do	کن	*kon*
مردن	*mordan*	to die	میر	*mīr.*

V. Verbs in ـندن -ndan

These reject the ـدن -dan for the root.

To this class belong, in addition to the causative verbs (§ 56 (b)) the following:

	Infinitive			Present Stem
افکندن	*afkandan*	to throw	افکن	*afkan*
پراکندن	*parākandan*	to scatter	پراکن	*parākan*
راندن	*rāndan*	to drive	ران	*rān*
کندن	*kandan*	to dig	کن	*kan*
ماندن	*māndan*	to remain	مان	*mān*.

VI. The following verbs in ـدن -dan preceded by a short vowel may for convenience' sake be grouped together:

	Infinitive			Present Stem
آمدن	*āmadan*	to come	آ	*ā*
زدن	*zadan*	to strike	زن	*zan*
ستدن	*setadan*	to take	ستن	*setan*
شدن	*šodan*	to become	شو	*šav-*, *šou̯*.

VII. Infinitives in ـختن -xtan.

These reject the خ x and substitute ز z:

	Infinitive			Present Stem
آموختن	*āmūxtan*	to teach	آموز	*āmūz*
آمیختن	*āmīxtan*	to mix	آمیز	*āmīz*
آویختن	*āvīxtan*	to hang	آویز	*āvīz*
افراختن	*afrāxtan*	to raise	افراز	*afrāz*
افروختن	*afrūxtan*	to kindle	افروز	*afrūz*
انداختن	*andāxtan*	to throw	انداز	*andāz*
اندوختن	*andūxtan*	to collect	اندوز	*andūz*
انگیختن	*angīxtan*	to excite	انگیز	*angīz*
باختن	*bāxtan*	to lose at play	باز	*bāz*
بیختن	*bīxtan*	to sift	بیز	*bīz*
پختن	*poxtan*	to cook	پز	*paz*
پرداختن	*pardāxtan*	to finish	پرداز	*pardāz*
تاختن	*tāxtan*	to assault	تاز	*tāz*
دوختن	*dūxtan*	to sew	دوز	*dūz*
ریختن	*rīxtan*	to pour	ریز	*rīz*
ساختن	*sāxtan*	to make	ساز	*sāz*
سوختن	*sūxtan*	to burn	سوز	*sūz*
گداختن	*godāxtan*	to melt	گداز	*godāz*
گریختن	*gorīxtan*	to flee	گریز	*gorīz*
نواختن	*navākhtan*	to caress	نواز	*navāz*.

Exceptions:

	Infinitive			Present Stem
دوختن	*dūxtan*	to milk	دوش	*dūš*
شناختن	*šenāxtan*	to know (*connaître*)	شناس	*šenās*
فروختن	*forūxtan*	to sell	فروش	*forūš*

VIII. Verbs in *-stan*

(a) verbs in ستن- *-estan*

These reject the ending for the root

	Infinitive			Present Stem
بایستن	*bāyestan*	to be necessary	بای	*bāy*
توانستن	*tavānestan*	to be able	توان	*tavān*
دانستن	*dānestan*	to know (*savoir*)	دان	*dān*
شایستن	*šāyestan*	to be possible	شای	*šāy*
مانستن	*mānestan*	to resemble	مان	*mān*
یارستن	*yārestan*	to be able	یار	*yār*

(b) Verbs in ستن- *-stan* in which the س *s* is part of the root.

These reject the س *s* and substitute ه *h*:

	Infinitive			Present Stem
جستن	*ǰastan*	to leap	جه	*jah*
خواستن	*xvāstan*	to wish	خواه	*xvāh*
رستن	*rastan*	to escape	ره	*rah*
کاستن	*kāstan*	to lessen	کاه	*kāh.*

(c) Miscellaneous:

	Infinitive			Present Stem
آراستن	*ārāstan*	to adorn	آرا	*ārā*
بستن	*bastan*	to bind	بند	*band*
پیراستن	*pīrāstan*	to adorn	پیرا	*pīrā*
پیوستن	*peịvastan*	to join	پیوند	*peịvand*
خاستن	*xāstan*	to rise	خیز	*xīz*
رستن	*rostan*	to grow	رو	*rū*
زیستن	*zīstan*	to live	زی	*zī*
شستن	*šostan*	to wash	شو	*šū*
شکستن	*šekastan*	to break	شکن	*šekan*
گریستن	*gerīstan*	to weep	گری	*gery*
گسستن	*gosestan*	to snap	گسل	*gosel*
نشاستن	*nešāstan*	to place	نشان	*nešān*
نشستن	*nešastan*	to sit	نشین	*nešīn*
نگریستن	*negarīstan*	to look	نگر	*negar.*

Note: In the colloquial language the present stem of نشستن *nešastan* is *šīn-*, *šin*. Ex.:

mīšine < مینشیند *mīnešīnad* he sits.

IX. Verbs in ـشتن *-štan*

These reject the ش *š* and substitute ر *r*:

	Infinitive			Present Stem
انباشتن	*anbāštan*	to fill	انبار	*anbār*
انگاشتن	*engāštan*	to think	انگار	*engār*
پنداشتن	*pendāštan*	to think	پندار	*pendār*
داشتن	*dāštan*	to have	دار	*dār*
کاشتن	*kāštan*	to sow	کار	*kār*
کشتن	*keštan*	to sow	کار	*kār*
گذاشتن	*gozāštan*	to put, let	گذار	*gozār*
گذشتن	*gozaštan*	to pass	گذر	*gozar*
گماشتن	*gomāštan*	to depute	گمار	*gomār*
نگاشتن	*negāštan*	to paint	نگار	*negār*

Exceptions:

افراشتن	*afrāštan*	to raise	افراز	*afrāz*
رشتن	*reštan*	to spin	ریس	*rīs*
سرشتن	*sereštan*	to mix	سریس	*serīs*
کشتن	*koštan*	to kill	کش	*koš*
گشتن	*gaštan*	to turn	گرد	*gard*
نوشتن	*neveštan*	to write	نویس	*nevīs*
هشتن	*heštan*	to leave	هل	*hel.*

Note: In the colloquial language گذاشتن *gozāštan* loses the initial syllable both in the past and present forms. Exx.:

nazār < نگذار *nagozar* do not let.
mīzāštam < میگذاشتم *mīgozāštam* I should let.

X. Verbs in ـفتن *-ftan*

These reject the ف *f* and substitute ب *b*:

	Infinitive			Present Stem
تافتن	*tāftan*	to twist	تاب	*tāb*
شتافتن	*šetāftan*	to hurry	شتاب	*šetāb*
فریفتن	*ferīftan*	to deceive	فریب	*ferīb*
کوفتن	*kūftan*	to beat	کوب	*kūb*
یافتن	*yāftan*	to find, to obtain	یاب	*yāb.*

The following insert ن *-n-*:

سفتن	*softan*	to bore	سنب	*sonb*
نهفتن	*nehoftan*	to hide	نهنب	*nehonb.*

Exceptions:

بافتن	*bāftan*	to weave	باف	*bāf*
پذیرفتن	*pazīroftan*	to receive	پذیر	*pazīr*
رفتن	*raftan*	to go	رو	*rav- rou̯*
شنفتن	*šenoftan*	to hear	شنو	*šenav- šenou̯*
کافتن	*kāftan*	to dig	کاو	*kāv*
گرفتن	*gereftan*	to take, seize	گیر	*gīr*
گفتن	*goftan*	to say	گو	*gū*.

Personal endings

§ 34. In the case of the tenses formed from the present stem the personal endings are as follows:

Pers.	Sing.		Plur.	
1.	ـم	*-am*	ـیم	*-īm*
2.	ی	*-ī*	ـید	*-īd*
3.	ـد	*-ad*	ـند	*-and*.

It should be noted however that the second singular of the imperative takes no ending and consists of the bare stem.
In the case of the tenses formed from the past stem the same endings are employed except that the third person singular of the imperative consists of the bare stem only.

Note. For ـید *-īd* the colloquial language substitutes ـین *-in*. Exx.:
dārin < دارید *dārīd* you have
raftin < رفتید *raftīd* you went.

Tenses from the Present Stem.

§ 35. From the present stem are formed the following four tenses:

1. Simple Present.

Pers.	Sing.		Plur.	
1.	پرسم	*porsam*	پرسیم	*porsīm*
2.	پرسی	*porsī*	پرسید	*porsīd*
3.	پرسد	*porsad*	پرسند	*porsand*.

2. Continuous Present, formed by prefixing the particle می *mī* to the Simple Present.

Pers.	Sing.		Plur.	
1.	می پرسم	*mī porsam*	می پرسیم	*mī porsīm*
2.	می پرسی	*mī porsī*	می پرسید	*mī porsīd*
3.	می پرسد	*mī porsad*	می پرسند	*mī porsand*.

3. Present Subjunctive, sometimes identical with the Simple Present, but usually with the prefixed particle بـ *be-* (§§ 5, *Note 2* and (c)(ii)).

Pers.		Sing.		Plur.
1.	بپرسم	*beporsam*	بپرسیم	*beporsīm*
2.	بپرسی	*beporsī*	بپرسید	*beporsīd*
3.	بپرسد	*beporsad*	بپرسند	*beporsand.*

4. Imperative, also usually with prefixed بِ *be-*, the 1st and 3rd persons being supplied from the Present Subjunctive. Note that the second person singular takes no ending (§ 34).

Pers.		Sing.		Plur.
1.	بپرسم	*beporsam*	بپرسیم	*beporsīm*
2.	بپرس	*bepors*	بپرسید	*beporsīd*
3.	بپرسد	*beporsad*	بپرسند	*beporsand.*

From the present stem are also formed the present participle in ـنده *-ande* and ـان *-ān.*

پرسنده *porsande*
پرسان *porsān.*

On the syntax of these forms see §§ 79, 80, 85, 86, 90 and 91.

Tenses from the Past Stem

§ 36. From the past stem are formed the following two tenses:

1. Simple Past.

Pers.		Sing.		Plur.
1.	پرسیدم	*porsīdam*	پرسیدیم	*porsīdīm*
2.	پرسیدی	*porsīdī*	پرسیدید	*porsīdīd*
3.	پرسید	*porsīd*	پرسیدند	*porsīdand.*

2. Continuous Past formed by prefixing the particle می *mī* to the Simple Past.

Pers.		Sing.		Plur.
1.	می پرسیدم	*mī porsīdam*	می پرسیدیم	*mī porsīdīm*
2.	می پرسیدی	*mī porsīdī*	می پرسیدید	*mī porsīdīd*
3.	می پرسید	*mī porsīd*	می پرسیدند	*mī porsīdand.*

On the syntax of these tenses see §§ 81 and 82.

From the past stem are also derived, in addition to the Infinitive (پرسیدن *porsīdan*), the Future Participle formed by adding ـی *-ī* to the Infinitive (پرسیدنی *porsīdanī*) the Short Infinitive (پرسید *porsīd*), identical in form with the third person singular of the Past Definite, and, with the addition of the ending ـه *-e*, the Past Participle (پرسیده *porside*). See §§ 88, 89, 92 and 93.

§ 37. With the Past Participle in conjunction with the relevant forms of the verb بودن *būdan* "to be" (§ 41, 1.) are formed the following compound tenses.

1. Perfect:

Pers.		Sing.		Plur.
1.	پرسیده ام	*porsīde am*	پرسیده ایم	*porsīde īm*
2.	پرسیده ای	*porsīde ī*	پرسیده اید	*porsīde īd*
3.	پرسیده است	*porsīde ast*	پرسیده اند	*porsīde and.*

Note: In the 3rd person singular است *ast* is frequently omitted.

2. Continuous Perfect, formed from the Perfect by prefixing the particle می *mi*:

Pers.		Sing.		Plur.
1.	می پرسیده ام	*mī porsīde am*	می پرسیده ایم	*mī porsīde īm*
2.	می پرسیده ای	*mī porsīde ī*	می پرسیده اید	*mī porsīde īd*
3.	می پرسیده است	*mī porsīde ast*	می پرسیده اند	*mī porsīde and.*

Note: Here too است *ast* is frequently omitted in the 3rd person singular.

3. Perfect Subjunctive.

Pers.		Sing.		Plur.
1.	پرسیده باشم	*porsīde bāšam*	پرسیده باشیم	*porsīde bāšīm*
2.	پرسیده باشی	*porsīde bāšī*	پرسیده باشید	*porsīde bāšīd*
3.	پرسیده باشد	*porsīde bāšad*	پرسیده باشند	*porsīde bāšand.*

4. Pluperfect:

Pers.		Sing.		Plur.
1.	پرسیده بودم	*porsīde būdam*	پرسیده بودیم	*porsīde būdīm*
2.	پرسیده بودی	*porsīde būdī*	پرسیده بودید	*porsīde būdīd*
3.	پرسیده بود	*porsīde būd*	پرسیده بودند	*porsīde būdand.*

On the syntax of these tenses see §§ 83, 84 and 87.

§ 38. The Future is formed by the Simple Present of خواستن *xvāstan* "to wish" (§ 33 8 (b)) followed by the Short Infinitive (§§ 36 and 89):

Pers.		Sing.		Plur.
1.	خواهم پرسید	*xvāham porsīd*	خواهیم پرسید	*xvāhīm porsīd*
2.	خواهی پرسید	*xvāhī porsīd*	خواهید پرسید	*xvāhīd porsīd*
3.	خواهد پرسید	*xvāhad porsīd*	خواهند پرسید	*xvāhand porsīd.*

§ 39. Passive: The Passive is expressed by means of the Past Participle followed by the relevant form of the verb شدن *šodan* "to become." Thus from کشتن *koštan* "to kill":

کشته می شود *košte mī šavad* he is being killed
کشته خواهد شد *košte xvāhad šod* he will be killed
کشته شد *košte šod* he was killed
کشته شده است *košte šode ast* he has been killed
کشته شده بود *košte šode būd* he had been killed.

گشتن *gaštan* (گردیدن *gardīdan*) may be used as a synonym of شدن *šodan.*

§ 40. Negation: Negation is expressed by prefixing the particle ن *na-* "not." Exx.

نپرسیدم *naporsīdam* I did not ask < پرسیدم *porsīdam* I asked
نرفت *naraft* he did not go < رفت *raft* he went
ندیدید *nadīdīd* you did not see < دیدید *dīdīd* you saw.

When the verb begins with a vowel a euphonic *-y-* is inserted:

نیامد *nayāmad* he did not come < آمد *āmad* he came.

ن *na-* precedes the particle می *mī* (§ 35, 2) and displaces the particle ب *be-* (§ 35, 3). Exx.:

نمیدانم *namīdānam* I do not know < میدانم *mīdānam* I know
نگوئید *nagū'īd* do not say < بگوئید *begū'īd* say
نرسد *narasad* let him not arrive < برسد *berasad* let him arrive.

In compound tenses (§ 37) ن *na-* precedes the past participle. Exx.:

ندیده ام *nadīde am* I have not seen < دیده ام *dīde am* I have seen
نرفته است *narafte ast* he has not gone < رفته است *rafte ast* he has gone
نگفته بودید *nagofte būdīd* you had not said < گفته بودید *gofte būdīd* you had said.

In the future (§ 38) it is prefixed to the auxiliary. Exx.:

نخواهم رفت *naxvāham raft* I shall not go < خواهم رفت *xvāham raft* I shall go
نخواهد دید *naxvāhad dīd* he will not see < خواهد دید *xvāhad dīd* he will see.

In the passive (§ 39) it is prefixed to the form of شدن *šodan* etc. Exx.:

کشته نشد *košte našod* he was not killed < کشته شد *košte šod* he was killed
دیده نمیشود *dīde namīšavad* it is not seen < دیده میشود *dīde mīšavad* it is seen.

In the case of verbal expressions (§ 60) it is prefixed to the verbal form. Exx.:

باز نمیکند *bāz namīkonad* he does not open < باز میکند *bāz mīkonad* he opens
در نرفتند *dar naraftand* they did not run away < در رفتند *dar raftand* they ran away
فراموش نمیکنم *farāmūš namīkonam* I do not forget < فراموش میکنم *farāmūš mīkonam* I forget.

Note 1: In Classical Persian the negation of the Imperative was expressed by means of the particle م *ma-*, which is still sometimes found in the literary language in place of the normal ن *na-*.

Note 2: On the negative forms of the present tense of بودن *būdan* "to be" see § 43.

§ 41. The verb بودن *būdan* "to be": The present tense of بودن *budan* is anomalous in that it has four different series of forms as shown below, all of which except the fourth series may be employed only in the Simple Present (§ 35.1).

1.

Pers.		Sing.		Plur.
1.	ام	*am*	ایم	*īm*
2.	ای	*ī*	اید	*īd*
3.	است	*ast*	اند	*and.*

These forms, which are enclitic, are usually attached to the previous word, in which case the initial *alef* disappears. They must however be written separately when the preceding word ends in a silent ه, and in such cases the second person (ای *ī*) is still usually represented by a *hamze* over the ه. Exx.:

سردست *sardast* it is cold
ممنونم *mamnūnam* I am grateful
خسته اند *xaste and* they are tired
بچّهٔ *bačče-ī* } thou art a child.
بچّه ای *bačče ī* }

Note: In the colloquial language *ast* when following a consonant is contracted to *e*. After a vowel it is represented by *s* (< *st*). Exx.:
xūbe it is good < *xūbast*
momkene it is possible < *momkenast*
gās perhaps < *gāh ast.*

2.

Pers.		Sing.		Plur.
1.	هستم	*hastam*	هستیم	*hastīm*
2.	هستی	*hastī*	هستید	*hastīd*
3.	هست	*hast*	هستند	*hastand.*

3.

Pers.		Sing.		Plur.
1.	بوم	*bovam*	بویم	*bovīm*
2.	بوی	*bovī*	بوید	*bovīd*
3.	بود	*bovad*	بوند	*bovand.*

Note 1: This series of forms is found only in poetry.

Note 2: From this stem is derived the isolated optative form باد *bād* (< *bovād*) "may (he) be" in such phrases as:

زنده باد شاه *zende bād šāh* long live the king! (*lit.* may the king be alive!)
مرده باد ظالم *morde bād zālem* down with the tyrant! (*lit.* may the tyrant be dead!)

4.

Pers.		Sing.		Plur.
1.	باشم	*bāšam*	باشيم	*bāšīm*
2.	باشى	*bāšī*	باشيد	*bāšīd*
3.	باشد	*bāšad*	باشند	*bāšand.*

These forms, unlike the preceding three series, are used to express the Subjunctive and the Imperative as well as the Indicative. As they do not admit of the prefix بِ *be-* the above forms represent both the Simple Present and the Subjunctive. The Continuous Present is expressed in the usual way by means of the prefix مى *mī*.

§ **42.** The Simple Past of بودن *būdan* is formed regularly:

Pers.		Sing.		Plur.
1.	بودم	*būdam*	بوديم	*būdīm*
2.	بودى	*būdī*	بوديد	*būdīd*
3.	بود	*būd*	بودند	*būdand.*

Since these forms do not admit of the prefix مى *mī* they do service for the Continuous Past also. For the same reason there is no Continuous Perfect (§ 31, 2), and the verb is likewise defective in having no Pluperfect.

Note: The forms ميبودم *mībūdam* etc. may occur in conditional sentences. See § 95. II(a) *Note.*

§ **43.** The negation of the forms ام *am* etc. (§ 41, 1) is regular except in the 3rd pers. sing.:

Pers.		Sing.		Plur.
1.	نيم	*nayam*	نئيم	*na'īm*
2.	نئى	*na'ī*	نئيد	*na'īd*
3.	نيست	*nīst*	نيند	*nayand.*

نيست *nist* is also the 3rd pers. sing. of the negative forms of هستم *hastam* etc. (§ 41, 2):

Pers.		Sing.		Plur.
1.	نيستم	*nīstam*	نيستيم	*nīstīm*
2.	نيستى	*nīstī*	نيستيد	*nīstīd*
3.	نيست	*nīst*	نيستند	*nīstand.*

In all other parts of the verb the negative forms are regular.

Note: On the analogy of نيستم *nīstam* etc. are formed the combinations كيستم *kīstam* "who am I?" etc. and چيستم *čīstam* "what am I?" etc. in which the first element is كه *ke* or كى *ki* "who?" and چه *če* "what?" respectively.

§ **44.** Impersonal Verbs: The Verbs بایستن *bāyestan* "to be necessary" and شایستن *šāyestān* "to be fitting," "to be possible" are used only in the 3rd pers. sing. بایستن *bāyestan* occurs normally in the Simple Present and Past, i.e. باید *bāyad* "it is necessary", "*il faut,*" and بایست *bāyest* "it was necessary," "*il fallait.*" However میباید *mībāyad* and میبایست *mībāyest* likewise occur, as also, as synonyms of the latter, the archaic forms بایستی *bāyestī* and میبایستی *mībāyestī.*

شایستن *šāyestan* occurs as a finite verb only in the 3rd pers. sing. of the Simple Present, i.e. شاید *šāyad* "it is fitting," "it is possible." The present participle in ان‍ـ *-ān* (§ 35) and the past participle are used adjectivally: شایان *šāyān* "fitting," "splendid," شایسته *šāyeste* "proper," "suitable."

Here too may be mentioned توان "it is possible" from the present stem of توانستن *tavānestan* "to be able" (§ 33, VIII(a)): there is also a Continuous Present, میتوان *mītavān,* and a Subjunctive form بتوان *betavān.*
On the syntax of these impersonal verbs see §§ 85 (c) and 89 (b).

§ **45.** Prepositions: The simple prepositions are as follows:

- از *az* from, out of
- با *bā* with
- بر *bar* on
- به *be,* بـ *be-* to
- بی *bī* without
- تا *tā* up to, until
- جز *ǰoz* except
- در *dar* in.

Note 1: به *be* "to" and در *dar* "in" are frequently omitted in the colloquial language, Exx.:

میروم تهران *mīravam tehrān* I am going to Tehran
منزل بودم *manzel būdam* I was at home.

Note 2: بی *bī* "without" occurs almost exclusively in such expressions as بی سر *bī sar* "headless;" otherwise its place is taken by the prepositional phrase بدون *bedūn-e.*

§ **46.** As a supplement to, and to some extent as a substitute for, the simple prepositions, the modern language has recourse to a great number of prepositional phrases, which fall into two main categories.

(a) The vast majority of these phrases are of the type of the English *in front of, on account of, because of,* etc., consisting of a noun or adverb preceded by a preposition and followed by the *eẓāfe.* The prepositions used most commonly are در *dar* "in" and بر *bar* "on," for which از *az* "from" and بـ *be* "to" can be substituted to indicate motion from or to the object respectively. The prepositions در *dar,* بر *bar* and بـ *be* are often omitted from the phrases in the written, and always in the spoken language. Exx.:

(در) بالایِ (*dar*) *bālā-ye* above, up < بالا *bālā* height

(در) بینِ (*dar*) *bei̯n-e* between, among < بین *bei̯n* interval

(در) پسِ (*dar*) *pas-e* behind < پس *pas* behind (adv.)

(در) پشتِ (*dar*) *pošt-e* behind < پشت *pošt* back

(در) پهلویِ (*dar*) *pahlū-ye* beside < پهلو *pahlū* side

(در) پیشِ (*dar*) *pīš-e* in front of, with (*chez*) < پیش *pīš* (in) front

(در) تویِ (*dar*) *tū-ye* in < تو *tū* inside

بجایِ *bejā-ye* instead of < جا *jā* place

(در) جلوِ (*dar*) *jelou̯-e* in front of < جلو *jelou̯* bridle, front

(در) دورِ (*dar*) *dou̯r-e* around, about < دور *dou̯r* circumference

(بر) رویِ (*bar*) *rū-ye* on < رو *rū* face

(در) زیرِ (*dar*) *zīr-e* under < زیر *zīr* underneath

(بر) سرِ (*bar*) *sar-e* on < سر *sar* head

(در) عوضِ (*dar*) *'evaẓ-e* instead of < عوض *'evaẓ* substitute

بمثلِ *bemeṣl-e* } like < مثل *meṣl* likeness
مثلِ *meṣle-e* }

(در) میانِ (*dar*) *miyān-e* between, among < میان *miyān* middle

با وجودِ *bā vojūd-e* in spite of < وجود *vojūd* existence.

Note. Here may also be included برایِ *barā-ye* "for" in which *ba-* represents the older pronunciation of the preposition به, بِ *be*, *be-* and *rā* is an old noun which now only survives as the particle used to indicate the accusative (§ 11); and همراهِ *hamrāh-e* "(along) with" < همراه *hamrāh* "fellow-traveller."

(b) A few of these phrases consist of an adverb or adjective followed by a simple preposition:

بعد *ba'd* afterwards > بعد از *ba'd az* after

پس *pas* then, afterwards > پس از *pas az* after

پیش *pīš* before, formerly > پیش از *pīš az* before

راجع *rāje'* referring > راجع ب *rāje' be* regarding, concerning

غیر *γei̯r* other, different > غیر از *γei̯r az* except

قبل *qabl* before, previously > قبل از *qabl az* before.

§ **47.** Adverbs: True adverbs such as اکنون *aknūn* "now," فردا *fardā* "to-morrow," کی *kei̯* "when?" are rare in Persian, the function of adverbs being assumed by:

(1) Adjectives. Exx.:

تند *tond* quickly < تند *tond* quick
خوب *xūb* well < خوب *xūb* good
روان *ravān* fluently < روان *ravān* fluent.

Note: The ending انه *-āne* (§ 55 (b)) frequently has an adverbial sense. Exx.: متأسفانه *mota'assefāne* "unfortunately," عاقلانه *'āqelāne* "wisely."

(2) Pronouns. The following except دیگر *dīgar* in the sense of "again" are employed only in negative sentences:

چندان *čandān* much, very < چندان *čandān* so much
دیگر *dīgar* again, any longer < دیگر *dīgar* other
هیچ *hīč* at all < هیچ *hīč* any.

(3) Nouns, which may occur either

(a) alone:

شب *šab* in the night < شب *šab* night
صبح *ṣobḥ* in the morning < صبح *ṣobḥ* morning
جلو *ǰelou̯* in front, forward < جلو *ǰelou̯* bridle, front

or

(b) defined by a pronominal adjective:

آنوقت *ānvaqt* then < آن *ān* that + وقت *vaqt* time
اینطور *inṭou̯r* thus < این *in* this + طور *ṭou̯r* manner
همه جا *hame ǰā* everywhere < همه *hame* all, every + جا *ǰā* place.

Note: Here belong امروز *emrūz* "to-day," امشب *emšab* "to-night" and امسال *emsāl* "this year," in which the first component represents an old demonstrative.

(4) Arabic adverbial accusatives, i.e. Arabic nouns or adjectives in the accusative case with *tanvin* (§ 6 (d)). Exx.:

اخیراً *axīran* recently < اخیر *axīr* recent
تقریباً *taqrīban* approximately < تقریب *taqrīb* approximation
کاملاً *kāmelan* completely < کامل *kāmel* complete
مثلاً *maṣalan* for example < مثل *maṣal* example
مخصوصاً *maxṣūṣan* specially < مخصوص *maxṣūṣ* special.

Note: In حالا *ḥālā* "now" < حال *ḥal* "condition, state" the *tanvin* has been dropped and the vowel lenghtened.

§ 48. Adverbs of quality are for the most part identical with the correspondent adjectives, e.g. تند *tond* "quick" and "quickly," روان *ravān* "fluent" and "fluently." Otherwise the Persian adverbs or parts of speech employed as such fall into the following main categories:

(1) Adverbs of place. Exx.:

آنجا *ānǰā* there
اینجا *inǰā* here
بالا *bālā* above, up
بیرون *bīrūn* outside, out
پائین *pā'in* down
پس *pas* behind, back
پشت *pošt* behind
تو *tū* inside
جلو *ǰelou̯* in front, forward
دور *dūr* far
زیر *zīr* underneath
عقب *'aqab* behind
نزدیک *nazdīk* near
همه جا *hame ǰā* everywhere.

Note: On the adverbial numerals see § 26, note 3.

(2) Adverbs of time. Exx.:

آنگاه *āngāh* } then
آنوقت *ānvaqt* }
اکنون *aknūn* now
امروز *emrūz* to-day
امسال *emsāl* this year
امشب *emšab* to-night
بارها *bārhā* often
باز *bāz* again
بعد *ba'd* after(wards)
پارسال *pārsāl* last year
پریروز *parīrūz* the day before yesterday
پریشب *parīšab* the night before last
پس *pas* then
پیرارسال *pīrārsal* the year before last
پیش *pīš* before
پیوسته *pei̯vaste* always
حالا *ḥālā* now
دو باره *do bāre* again
دیر *dīr* late
دیروز *dīrūz* yesterday
دیشب *dīšab* last night
زود *zūd* early
سابقاً *sābeqan* formerly
فردا *fardā* to-morrow
فوراً *fou̯ran* immediately
قبل *qabl* before
کنون *konūn* now
گاهی *gāhī* sometimes

ناگاه *nāgāh* unexpectedly
هرگز *hargez* (with negative verb) never
همواره *hamvāre* }
همیشه *hamīše* } always
هنوز *hanūz* still, yet.

(3) Adverbs of quantity and comparison. Exx.:

آنطور *ānṭou̯r* }
اینطور *inṭou̯r* } thus

اقلاً *aqallan* at least
بسیار *besyār* much, very
تنها *tanhā* only
چندان *čandān* so much, very much
حتی *ḥattā* even
زیاد *ziyād* much
فقط *faqaṭ* only
کم *kam* little.

(4) Adverbs of affirmation and negation. Exx.:

آری *ārī* yes
البته *albatte* of course
بلی *balī* yes
خیر *xei̯r* (نه خیر *na xei̯r*) no
شاید *šāyad* }
گویا *gūyā* } perhaps
نه *na* no, not.

Note 1: The colloquial forms of آری *ārī* and بلی *balī* are آره *āre* and بله *bale*.

Note 2: Strictly speaking شاید *šāyad* is the 3rd pers. sing., Simple Present, of شایستن *šayestan* "to be possible," on which see § 44. On the syntax of شاید *šāyad* and گویا *gūyā* in the sense of "perhaps" see § 85(c) and Notes 1 and 2.

(5) Adverbs of interrogation. Exx.:

چرا *čerā* why?
چطور *četou̯r* how?
چقدر *čeqadr* how much?
چگونه *čegūne* how?
چند *čand* how much?
کجا *koǰā* where?
کی *kei̯* when?

Note: On the accentuation of چرا *čerā* see § 7(d), note 2.

§ 49. Many adverbs admit of the comparative ending in *-tar* (§ 15):

بالاتر *bālātar* higher up < بالا *bālā* up, above
پیشتر *pīštar* formerly < پیش *pīš* before
جلوتر *ǰelou̯tar* further forward < جلو *ǰelou̯* in front, forward.

§ 50. Conjunctions: The simple conjunctions are as follows:

آیا *āyā nonne?*
اگر *agar* if
اگرچه *agarče* although
اما *ammā* but
پس *pas* therefore
تا *tā* until, in order that, so long as
چون *čūn* as, since
چه *če* because
... چه ... چه *če* ... *če* ... both ... and ...
... خواه ... خواه *xvāh* ... *xvāh* ... either ... or ...
زیرا *zīrā* because
که *ke* that
مگر *magar* except; *num?*
نیز *nīz* also
و *o, va* and
ولی *valī* } but
ولیکن *valīkan* }
هم *ham* also
... هم ... هم *ham* ... *ham* ... both ... and ...
یا *yā* or
... یا ... یا *yā* ... *yā* ... either ... or ...

Note: On the syntax of اگر *agar*, see § 95.
و *o* is used to connect words and و *va* to connect sentences. However, in the colloquial language و *o* is used in all cases.
On که *ke* see §§ 97 and 98.

§ 51. In addition to the simple conjunctions the modern language makes use of a great number of conjunctival phrases, which fall into the three following categories:

(a) A pronoun, preposition, adverb or conjunction is followed by the conjunction که *ke* "that." Exx.:

بل *bal* nay > بلکه *balke* but (after a negative)
چرا *čerā* why? > چراکه *čerāke* because
چندان *čandān* so much > چندانکه *čandānke* as much as
چون *čūn* as, since > چونکه *čūnke* because
زیرا *zīrā* because > زیراکه *zīrāke* because
همین *hamin* (the) same > همینکه *haminke* as soon as.

Note: Here may be also mentioned چنانچه *čonānče* "if" < چنان *čonān* "such" + the relative چه *če*; هرگاه *har gāh* "whenever, if" < هر *har* "every" + گاه *gāh* "time;" and هر وقت *har vaqt* "whenever" < هر *har* + وقت *vaqt* "time."

(b) A preposition or prepositional phrase is followed by the pronous این *in* "this" or آن *ān* "that" followed in turn by the conjunction که *ke*, the two words being usually written as one, i.e. اینکه *īnke*, آنکه *ānke*. Exx.:

با وجودِ *bā vojūd-e* in spite of > با وجود اینکه *bā vojūd-e inke* although
برایِ *barā-ye* for > برایِ اینکه *barā-ye inke* because, in order that
بعد از *ba'd az* after > بعد از آنکه *ba'd az ānke* after
پیش از *pīš az* before > پیش از آنکه *pīš az ānke* before
تا *tā* until, in order that > تا اینکه *tā inke* in order that
مثلِ *mesl-e* like > مثلِ اینکه *mesl-e inke* as though.

Note: Certain of these conjunctival phrases govern the subjunctive. See § 85 (g).

(c) A noun, usually governed by a preposition, takes the relative suffix ى *-ī* (§§ 23 and 98) followed by the conjunction كه *ke*, which is usually written as part of the word. Exx.:

صورت *ṣūrat* face, case > در صورتیکه *dar ṣūratīke* in case
طور *tour* manner, way > بطوریکه *betourīke* as
وقت *vaqt* time > وقتیکه *vaqtīke* when.

§ 52 (a) Interjections: True interjections are:

آهای *āhāi* hey!
ای *ei* O!
اوه *ūh* oh!
به به *bah bah* bravo!
وای *vāi* alas!

(b) The following are original substantives used as interjections:

آفرین *āferin* bravo! (*lit.* praise)
افسوس *afsūs* alas! (*lit.* regret)
تف *tof* fie! (*lit.* spittle)
حیف *ḥeif* what a pity! (*lit.* injustice)
عجب *'ajab* how strange! fancy! (*lit.* wonder).

In addition

(c) Certain Arabic phrases are used with the force of interjections:

استغفر الله *astaγfero'llah* Heaven forbid! (*lit.* I ask pardon of God)
الحمد لله *alḥamdo lillāh* Thank heaven! (*lit.* the praise [belongs] to God)
ان شاء الله *en šā'a'llāh* God willing (*lit.* if God will)
بارک الله *bāraka'llah* bravo! (*lit.* may God bless [you]!)
یاالله *yā'llāh* get up! hurry up! (*lit.* O God!)

Derivation and Composition

§ 53. Suffixes: Persian is comparatively rich in nominal and adjectival suffixes. The following lists include only such as are still productive in the modern language or occur in the formation of common words; suffixes dealt with in §§ 12, 13, 15, and 17 have been omitted.

§ 54. The following suffixes are used in the formation of nouns:

(a) ـار *-ār* added to the past stem of certain verbs forms a kind of verbal noun. Exx.:

دیدار *dīdār* visit > دیدن *dīdan* to see
کردار *kerdār* action > کردن *kardan* to do
گفتار *goftār* speech > گفتن *goftan* to say.

Note: In خریدار *xarīdār* "buyer" < خریدن *xarīdan* "to buy" the suffix retains its original function of forming *nomina agentis*. In گرفتار *gereftār* "captured" < گرفتن *gereftan* "to take" it has acquired a passive meaning.

(b) ـبان *-bān* conveys the idea of "keeper." Exx.:

باغبان *bāγbān* gardener < باغ *bāγ* garden
دربان *darbān* door-keeper < در *dar* door.

(c) ـچه *-če* is used to form diminutives. Exx.:

باغچه *bāγče* little garden < باغ *bāγ* garden
کتابچه *ketābče* notebook < کتاب *ketāb* book.

(d) ـچی *-čī*, a Turkish suffix, is increasingly used to denote the agent. Exx.:

تلگرافچی *telgerāfčī* telegraphist < تلگراف *telgerāf* telegram
شکارچی *šekārčī* hunter < شکار *šekār* hunting.

(e) ـدان *-dān* indicates the receptacle. Exx.:

قلمدان *qalamdān* pencase < قلم *qalam* pen
نمکدان *namakdān* salt-cellar < نمک *namak* salt.

(f) ـستان *-estān, -stān* forms nouns of place. Exx.:

افغانستان *afγānestān* Afghanistan < افغان *afγān* Afghan
نارنجستان *nāranǰestān* orange grove < نارنج *nāranǰ* orange.

(g) ـش *-eš*, added to the present stem of verbs, is used to form nouns of action. Exx.:

افرینش *āferīneš* creation < آفریدن *āferīdan* to create
خواهش *xvāheš* request < خواستن *xvāstan* to wish, to request.

(h) ـک *-ak* forms diminutives. Exx.:

اطاقک *oṭāqak* little room, cell < اطاق *oṭāq* room
دخترک *doxtarak* little girl < دختر *doxtar* girl, daughter
عروسک *'arūsak* doll < عروس *'arūs* bride.

(i) ـگر *-gar* denotes the agent. Exx.:

آهنگر *āhangar* blacksmith < آهن *āhan* iron
زرگر *zargar* goldsmith < زر *zar* gold
کارگر *kārgar* worker < کار *kār* work.

(j) ـه *-e* forms nouns, mostly concrete in sense, from nouns, adjectives and numerals. Exx.:

چشمه *čašme* spring < چشم *čašm* eye
دسته *daste* handle, group < دست *dast* hand
سفیده *sefīde* white of egg < سفید *sefīd* white
هفته *hafte* week < هفت *haft* seven.

Note: On ـه *-e* as a kind of definite article see § 8, *note*. On ـه *-e* as an adjectival suffix see § 55.

(k) ـی *-ī* forms abstract nouns. Exx.:

بزرگی *bozorgī* greatness < بزرگ *bozorg* great
خوبی *xūbī* goodness < خوب *xūb* good
مردی *mardī* manliness < مرد *mard* man.

Note 1: Silent ه *h* becomes گ *g* before this suffix as before the plural suffix ـان *-ān* (§ 12 (a)). Exx.:

بچّگی *baččegī* childhood < بچه *bačče* child
خستگی *xastegī* fatigue < خسته *xaste* tired
زندگی *zendegī* life < زنده *zende* alive.

Note 2: On the relative suffix ـی *-ī* see §§ 23 and 98. On ـی *-ī* as an adjectival suffix see § 55(h).

§ 55. The following suffixes are used in the formation of adjectives:

(a) ـا *-ā*, no longer productive, is added to the present stem of certain verbs:

توانا *tavānā* powerful < توان *tavān* < توانستن *tavānestan* to be able
دانا *dānā* wise < دان *dān* < دانستن *dānestan* to know.

(b) ـانه *-āne* is added to both nouns and adjectives and is usually applicable only to things, not to persons. Exx.:

دوستانه *dūstāne* friendly < دوست *dūst* friend
روزانه *rūzāne* daily < روز *rūz* day
عاقلانه *ʿāqelāne* intelligent < عاقل *ʿāqel* intelligent
محرمانه *maḥramāne* confidential < محرم *maḥram* confidant.

Note 1: Silent ه *h* becomes گ *g* before this suffix as before the plural ending ـان *-ān* (§ 12 (a)). Exx.:

بچّگانه *baččegāne* childish < بچّه *bačče* child.

Note 2: On the adverbial use of ـانه *-āne* see § 47 (1).

(c) ـمند *-mand* indicates the possession of a thing or quality. Exx.:

ثروتمند *s̱arvatmand* wealthy < ثروت *s̱arvat* wealth
خردمند *xeradmand* wise < خرد *xerad* wisdom
نیرومند *nīrūmand* strong < نیرو *nīrū* strength.

(d) ـناک *-nāk* forms adjectives of quality. Exx.:

خطرناک *xaṭarnāk* dangerous < خطر *xaṭar* danger
دردناک *dardnāk* painful < درد *dard* pain
نمناک *namnāk* damp < نم *nam* dampness.

(e) ـوار *-vār* denotes possession of a thing or quality and also fitness for a person. Exx.:

امیدوار *omīdvār* hopeful < امید *omīd* hope
شاهوار *šāhvār* royal, fit for a king < شاه *šāh* king.

(f) ـور *-var* denotes possession of a thing or quality. Exx.:

جانور *ǰānvar* animal (possessed of life) < جان *ǰān* soul, life
سخنور *soxanvar* eloquent < سخن *soxan* word
نامور *nāmvar* famous < نام *nām* name.

(g) ـه *-e* is added to possessive compounds (§ 60 (c)) of which the first element is a numeral. Exx.:

پنج ساله *panǰ sāle* five years old < پنج *panǰ* five + سال *sāl* year
دوچرخه *do čarxe* bicycle < دو *do* two + چرخ *čarx* wheel.

Note: Cf. also هر روزه *har rūze* "daily" < هر *har* "every" + روز *rūz* "day" and چه کاره *če kāre* "of what profession?" < چه *če* "what?" and کار *kār* "work."

(h) ـی *-ī*, by far the most productive of the adjectival suffixes, indicates relationship in the widest sense. Exx.:

آبی *ābī* watery; blue < آب *āb* water
ایرانی *īrānī* Persian < ایران *īrān* Persia
چوبی *čūbī* wooden < چوب *čūb* wood
شهری *šahrī* belonging to the town, urban < شهر *šahr* town
طلائی *ṭelā'ī* golden < طلا *ṭelā* gold
کمکی *komakī* auxiliary < کمک *komak* help.

Note: Silent ه *h* becomes گ *g* before this suffix. Ex.:
خانگی *xānegī* domestic < خانه *xāne* house.

(i) ـین *-in* forms adjectives of material. Exx.:

پشمین *pašmin* woollen < پشم *pašm* wool
زرین *zarrin* golden < زر *zar* gold
سیمین *sīmin* silver(y) < سیم *sīm* silver.

Note 1: This suffix has now been almost entirely displaced by ـی *-ī*, e.g. پشمی *pašmī* instead of the older پشمین *pašmīn*. Note also سنگین *sangīn* "heavy" < سنگ *sang* "stone" > سنگی *sangī* "stony, of stone."

§ **56.** Of the verbal suffixes only the two following are still to some extent productive:

(a) ـید *-īd* (infinitive in ـیدن *-īdan*, § 33 I) forms a few denominative verbs. Exx.:

دزدیدن *dozdīdan* to steal < دزد *dozd* thief
نامیدن *nāmīdan* to name < نام *nām* name.

In the following cases the suffix is added to Arabic verbal nouns:

بلعیدن *bal'īdan* to swallow < بلع *bal'* (act of) swallowing
رقصیدن *raqṣīdan* to dance < رقص *raqṣ* (act of) dancing
فهمیدن *fahmīdan* to understand < فهم *fahm* (act of) understanding.

(b) ـان *-ān* (infinitive in ـاندن *-āndan*, § 33 V, or ـانیدن *-ānīdan*, § 33 I) is added to the present stem to form causative verbs. Exx.:

ترساندن *tarsāndan* to frighten < ترس *tars* < ترسیدن *tarsīdan* to fear
سوزاندن *sūzāndan* to burn (tr.) < سوز *sūz* < سوختن *sūxtan* to burn (intr.)
گذراندن *gozarāndan* to cause to pass < گذر *gozar* < گذشتن *gozaštan* to pass.

Prefixes

§ 57. Only the two following prefixes are still productive:

(a) نا *nā-* corresponding to the English *un-* or *in-*, is attached to adjectives, nouns and verbals. Exx.:

نا پاک *nā pāk* impure < پاک *pāk* pure
نا خوش *nā xoš* unwell, ill < خوش *xoš* good
نا دان *nā dān* ignorant < دان *dān* < دانستن *dānestan* to know
نا مرد *nā mard* coward < مرد *mard* man.

Note: The prefix has a privative sense in ناامید *nā omīd* "hopeless" < امید *omīd* "hope" and نا باک *nā bāk* "fearless" < باک *bāk* "fear."

(b) هم *ham*, meaning "same," is attached to nouns to form what are in effect possessive compounds (§ 58 (c)). Exx.:

همراه *hamrāh* fellow-traveller (lit. of the same road) < راه *rāh* road
همسایه *hamsāye* neighbour (lit. having the same shadow) < سایه *sāye* shadow
هم عقیده *ham 'aqīde* of the same belief < عقیده *'aqīde* belief
هم وطن *ham vaṭan* compatriot (lit. of the same country) < وطن *vaṭan* country.

Note: On همراه *hamrāh-e* in the same of "(along) with" see § 46 (a) note.

Compounds

§ 58. Nouns and Adjectives: Persian is very rich in compound nouns and adjectives, of which there are three kinds.

(a) Determinative compounds are nouns in which the first element qualifies or determines the second. Exx.:

آزمایشگاه *āzmāyeshgāh* laboratory < آزمایش *āzmāyesh* experiment + گاه *gāh* place
پنبه‌دان *panbe-dān* cotton-seed < پنبه *panbe* cotton + دان *dān* seed
روزنامه *rūznāme* newspaper < روز *rūz* day + نامه *nāme* book
کارخانه *kārxāne* factory < کار *kār* work + خانه *xāne* house
گاو آهن *gāv-āhan* ploughshare < گاو *gāv* ox + آهن *āhan* iron.

(b) Objective compounds are adjectives or nouns of which the first element is a noun governed by the second, which is usually a verbal (identical in form with the present stem of the verb) and sometimes a past participle. Exx.:

آبکش *ābkaš* water-carrier < آب *āb* water + کش *kaš* < کشیدن *kašīdan* to draw
چادر نشین *čādor-nešīn* tent-dweller, nomad < چادر *čādor* tent + نشین *nešin* < نشستن *nešastan* to sit
دانشجو *dānešǰū* student < دانش *dāneš* knowledge + جو *ǰū* < جستن *ǰostan* to seek
سرمایه دار *sarmāye-dār* capitalist < سرمایه *sarmāye* capital + دار *dār* < داشتن *dāštan* to have
شاهزاده *šāhzāde* prince < شاه *šāh* king + زاده *zāde* born
هوا پیما *havā-peịmā* aeroplane < هوا *havā* air + پیما *peịmā* < پیمودن *peịmūdan* to traverse.

(c) Possessive compounds are adjectives or nouns, of which the first element qualifies the second (as in the case of determinative compounds) and the whole denotes a quality or attribute belonging to some person or thing. Exx.:

آهو چشم *āhū-čašm* having gazelle's eyes < آهو *āhū* gazelle + چشم *čašm* eye
خرگوش *xargūš* hare, *lit.* (animal) having donkey's ears < خر *xar* donkey + گوش *gūš* ear
خشبو *xošbū* fragrant < خوش *xoš* pleasant + بو *bū* smell
شش گوشه *šeš-gūše* hexagonal < شش *šeš* six + گوشه *gūše* corner
فارسی زبان *fārsī-zabān* Persian-speaking < فارسی *fārsī* Persian + زبان *zabān* tongue, language.

§ 59. In addition to these true compounds the following types of nominal and adjectival phrases perform the same function and may be regarded as a kind of loose compound:

(a) Two nouns are joined by the conjunction و *o* "and" to express a single idea. Exx.:

آب و هوا *āb o havā* climate < آب *āb* water + هوا *havā* air
مرز و بوم *marz o būm* country < مرز *marz* frontier + بوم *būm* region.

The two nouns are usually verbals, identical with the past and present stems of the verb, and may be

(i) both stems of the same verb:

جست و جو *ǰost o ǰū* search < جستن *ǰostan* to seek
شست و شو *šost o šū* (act of) washing < شستن *šostan* to wash
گفت و گو *goft o gū* conversation < گفتن *goftan* to say;

(ii) the past stems of two different verbs:

آمد و رفت *āmad o raft* traffic, intercourse < آمدن *āmadan* to come + رفتن *raftan* to go
داد و ستد *dād o setad* trade, barter < دادن *dādan* to give + ستدن *setadan* to take;

(iii) the past stem of one verb and the present of another:

جست و خیز *ǰast o xīz* leap, gambol < جستن *ǰastan* to leap + خاستن *xāstan* to rise
خرید و فروش *xarīd o forūš* trade < خریدن *xarīdan* to buy + فروختن *forūxtan* to sell;

or (iv) the present stems of two verbs:

گیر و دار *gīr o dār* brawl, uproar < گرفتن *gereftan* to seize + داشتن *dāštan* to hold.

(b) Two nouns or a noun and adjective are joined by the *eẓāfe* (§§ 11 (b) and 14):

تختِ خواب *taxt-e xvāb* bedstead < تخت *taxt* seat + خواب *xvāb* sleep
تخمِ مرغ *toxm-e morγ* egg < تخم *toxm* seed + مرغ *morγ* bird, fowl
راهِ آهن *rāh-e āhan* railway < راه *rāh* road + آهن *āhan* iron
سیبِ زمینی *sīb-e zamīnī* potato < سیب *sīb* apple + زمینی *zamīnī* (pertaining to the) earth
گلِ سرخ *gol-e sorx* rose < گل *gol* flower + سرخ *sorx* red.

Note 1: As the first element of nominal phrases سوء *sū'* "evil" and عدم *'adam* "non-existence" have the force of the English prefixes *mis-* and *non-*, *in-*, etc. respectively. Exx.:

سوءِ تفاهم *sū'-e tafāhom* misunderstanding < تفاهم *tafāhom* mutual understanding
سوءِ معامله *sū'-e mo'āmele* misuse, abuse < معامله *mo'āmele* treatment
عدمِ توجه *'adam-e tavaǰǰoh* inattention < توجّه *tavaǰǰoh* attention
عدمِ موافقت *'adam-e movāfeqat* disagreement < موافقت *movāfeqat* agreement.

Note 2: As the first element of adjectival phrases غیر *γeịr* "other" represents the English prefixes *un-*, *in-* etc. and قابل *qābel* "capable" the suffixes *-ible*, *-able*. Exx.:

غیرِ قانونی *γei̯r-e qānūnī* illegal < قانونی *qānūnī* legal
غیر ممکن *γei̯r-e momken* impossible < ممکن *momken* possible
غیرِ مستقیم *γei̯r-e mostaqīm* indirect < مستقیم *mostaqīm* direct
قابلِ تحمل *qābel-e taḥammol* endurable < تحمل *taḥammol* endurance
قابلِ تقسیم *qābel-e taqsīm* divisible < تقسیم *taqsīm* division
غیرِ قابلِ تقسیم *γei̯r-e qābel-e taqsīm* indivisible.

(c) Many adjectival phrases are formed with the preposition با *bā* "with;" the substitution of بی *bī* "without" has the force of the English *un-*, *in-*, etc. Exx.:

با ادب *bā adab* polite
بی ادب *bī adab* impolite < ادب *adab* politeness

با سواد *bā savād* literate
بی سواد *bī savād* illiterate < سواد *savād* literacy

با هوش *bā hūš* conscious
بی هوش *bī hūš* unconscious < هوش *hūš* consciousness.

§ **60.** Verbal Expressions: To make up for a deficiency in simple verbs the Persian language makes use of a great number of verbal expressions, which fall into two main classes. These are:

(a) Adverbial phrases, in which an adverb or preposition precedes and defines the verb. Exx.:

بر داشتن *bar dāštan* to lift up
پس دادن *pas dādan* to give back
در آوردن *dar āvordan* to pull out.

(b) Nominal phrases consisting of a noun or adjective governed by a verb, most frequently کردن *kardan* "to make." Such phrases, which are increasingly common in modern Persian, perform the function of our denominatives and are also used to convey ideas expressed in other languages by means of a primitive verb. Exx.:

بلند کردن *boland kardan* to raise (*lit.* to make high)
تغییر دادن *tayyīr dādan* to change (*lit.* to give a change)
زانو زدن *zānū zadan* to kneel (*lit.* to strike the knees)
سیاه کردن *siyāh kardan* to blacken (*lit.* to make black)
گم کردن *gom kardan* to lose (*lit.* to make lost)
منع کردن *manʿ kardan* to prohibit (*lit.* to make prohibition)
وعده دادن *vaʿde dādan* to promise (*lit.* to give a promise)
یاد دادن *yād dādan* to teach (*lit.* to give memory)
یاد داشتن *yād dāštan* to remember (*lit.* to have memory).

Note 1: For کردن *kardan* may be substituted, in the literary language, نمودن *namūdan lit.* "to show" and, in polite parlance, فرمودن *farmūdan lit.* "to command." Adjectival phrases also admit of the substitutes ساختن *sāxtan* "to make, manufacture" and گردانیدن *gardānīdan* "to cause to become."

Note 2: The passive of the nominal phrases is formed by substituting شدن *šodan* "to become" (and, in the literary language, گشتن *gaštan* or گردیدن *gardīdan* "to turn, become") for کردن *kardan* etc., and گرفتن *gereftan* "to take" and یافتن *yāftan* "to find" for دادن *dādan* "to give."

Syntax

The Sentence

§ 61. Order of Words: The normal word order in a simple sentence is subject, object or complement, verb. Adverbs or adverbial phrases precede or follow the object or complement. Exx.:

gāv-e māde šīr mīdehad The cow gives milk.
āb sar-čašme-ye zendegī ast Water is the source of life.
havā dar tābestān garm mīšavad The weather becomes hot in summer.
āftāb mīve-hā rā zūd mīrasānad The sun quickly ripens the fruit.
bād az panbe-zār yak panbe-dāne āvord (S) The wind brought a cottonseed from the cotton field.

Note 1: On complex sentences see below §§ 95–8.

Note 2: The following type of anacoluthon is common, particularly in the spoken language. The psychological subject stands at the head of the sentence, followed by the grammatical subject if expressed, and is then taken up by a suffixed pronoun in the body of the sentence. Exx.:

pīre zan delaš beḥāl-e xare sūxt (S) The old woman was sorry for the donkey. (*Lit.*, "The old woman, her heart burnt for the donkey's condition.")
manūčehr besyār garmaš būd Manūčehr was very hot. (*Lit.*, "Manūčehr, it was very hot to him.")
man az moḥīṭ-e madrase xei̯lī xoš-am mīāyad (D) I like the atmosphere of the school. (*Lit.*, I, it goes to me very well from the atmosphere of the school.)

Note 3: In the colloquial language adverbial phrases, especially if expressing direction, may be placed after the verb. Exx.:

gorge yaksar raft be āsiyāb va dastaš rā zad tū-y-e kīse-ye ārd (S) The wolf went straight away to the mill and put its paw in a sack of flour.
boz āmad bexāne-ye xodaš va az ānǰā raft beṣaḥrā (S) The goat came to its own house and went from there into the open country.
gonǰešk pārče-hā rā bar dāšt va āvord pahlū-y-e darzī (S) The sparrow picked up the pieces of cloth and brought them to the tailor.

Note 4: An attributive adjective sometimes follows the verb. See below, § 69, Note.

§ 62. The object is sometimes, for the sake of emphasis, placed before the subject. In English the same effect is achieved by the use of a passive construction. Exx.:

bīštar-e kār-e xāne rā to mīkonī Most of the housework is done by you.
kūh o ṣaḥrā rā barf gereft Mountain and plain are covered with snow.
in neʿmat-e bozorg rā xodā dāde ast This great blessing has been given by God.
mehrak rā in ḥarf gereft (S) Mehrak was affected by these words.

§ 63. Concord of Subject and Verb: Subject and verb agree in person and number except in the following cases:

(a) When a plural subject relates to inanimate things it normally takes a singular verb. Exx.:

dar zamestān rūzhā kūtāh ast In winter the days are short (*lit.* is) short.
γeẕā o āb o havā barā-ye zendegī lāzem ast Food, water and air (*lit.* is) necessary for life.
parhā-ye dom-e šotor morγ zībā ast The tail feathers of the ostrich are (*lit.* is) beautiful.

Note: However, when the subject consists of things which are thought of as separate entities or it is desired to stress their plurality, a plural verb may be used. Ex.:

xoršīd o māh o tamām-e setāregānī ke dar āsmān mī bīnīm kore-hā-ye besyār bozorgand The sun and moon and all the stars we see in the sky are very large globes.

(b) In polite language a subject denoting a single person may be followed by a plural verb. Exx.:

pādšāh bā doxtarešān piyāde šodand The king got out with his daughter.
safīr-e kabīr-e doulat-e englestān parīrūz ostovārnāme-ye ǰadīd-e xod rā beḥoẓūr-e šāh taqdīm kardand The British ambassador presented his new credentials to the Shah the day before yesterday.
vazīr-e moxtār-e belžīk emrūz beṭaraf-e brūksel ḥarakat namūdand The Belgian minister plenipotentiary left for Brussels to-day.

(c) When the subject is part of a larger whole there is a tendency to make the verb agree in person and number with the whole. Exx.:

aγlab man bā yakī do nafar az rofaqā nešaste būdīm Usually I was sitting with one or two of my friends.
šarṭ bebandīm tā kodām yak az mā beān deraxtī ke bālā-ye tape ast zūdtar mīrasīm Let us have a bet as to which of us is the first to reach the tree on the top of the hill.
baʿẓī az šomā čand martabe nāxoš šode īd Some of you have been ill several times.
ṣad tā γulām-e siyāh ke har kodāmešān bā ṣad nafar barābarand bīrūn mīāyand (S) A hundred black slaves, each of whom is equal to a hundred people, will come out.

Nouns

§ **64.** Use of *rā*: The definite object of the verb is usually followed by the particle *rā*. Exx.:

ketāb rā bemard dādam I gave the man the book.
asb rā dīdam I saw the horse.
gandom rā beāsyā bordand They took the wheat to the mill.

Note 1: If the object consists of two or more nouns connected by *o* "and" or if it is connected by the *eẓāfe* (§§ 11 (6) and 14) with a following noun, pronoun or adjective, the *rā* is placed at the end of the whole phrase. Exx.:

xāne o bāγ rā forūxtam I sold the house and the garden,
mard o zan o bačče rā dīdam I saw the man, woman and child.
bačče-ye-āhū rā mī gīrand They catch the young of the gazelle.
sar-e xod rā boland kard He raised his head.
bād barghā-ye xošk rā behar ṭaraf mībarad The wind blows the dry leaves in every direction.

Note 2: On *rā* attracted to the subject of the sentence see below § 98, *Note*.

§ **65.** The indefinite object does not usually take *rā*, which may however be added to give greater precision. Exx.:

sangī bar dāšt He picked up a stone.
ẓarfī por az āb āvord He brought a pot full of water.
az pūl-e māde gāv zamīnī xarīd He bought a piece of land with the money for the cow.
bošqāb-e sardī rā ǰelou̯-e boxār-e samāvar begīrīd Hold a cold saucer in front of the steam from the samovar.

§ **66.** The *eẓāfe*: The *eẓāfe* (§ 11 (b)) is used

(a) like the English preposition *of* to express the genitive relation. Exx.:

asb-e mard The man's horse (The horse of the man)
xāne-ye tāǰer The merchant's house (The house of the merchant)
barghā-ye deraxt The leaves of the tree.

(b) to connect geographical names with the word to which they stand in apposition (like *of* except in the case of rivers). Exx.:

kešvar-e īrān The country of Persia
šahr-e tehrān The city of Tehran.
rūd-e nīl The River Nile.

(c) to connect a personal name with a descriptive epithet. Exx.:

ʿīsā-ye masīḥ Jesus the Messiah.
mūsā-ye pei̯yambar The Prophet Moses.
ḥasan-e tāǰer Ḥasan the merchant.

Note: With the use described under (c) cf. the use of the *eẓāfe* to connect an attributive adjective with the noun it defines (§§ 14 and 69). Cf. also the use of the *eẓāfe* after *āqā* "master" in the sense of "Mr." and *marḥūm* "deceased." Exx.:

āqā-ye esfandiyārī Mr. Esfandiyārī.
marḥūm-e pedaram My late father.

§ **67.** The *eẓāfe* is omitted.

(a) in phrases with the words *sar* "head, end" and *ṣāḥeb* "master, owner" as the first element. Exx.:

sar angošt finger-tip < *angošt* finger.
sar čašme spring, source < *čašme* spring, fountain.
sar ḥadd frontier < *ḥadd* boundary.
ṣāḥeb xāne house-owner < *xāne* house.
ṣāḥeb māl proprietor, owner < *māl* property.

(b) in names of relations. Exx.:

pedar zan father-in-law < *pedar* father + *zan* wife.
pesar ʿammū nephew < *pesar* son + *ʿammū* (paternal) uncle.
doxtar berādar niece < *doxtar* daughter + *berādar* brother.

(c) after measures of quantity. Exx.:

do kīlo nān two kilos of bread.
yak līvān āb a tumbler of water.
se joft jūrāb three pairs of stockings.

(d) after words meaning "kind, sort." Exx.:

in qabīl mardom this kind of people.
in nouʿ jānvar this species of animal.

Note: In the colloquial language the *eẓāfe* is more frequently omitted especially is set phrases (§ 59 (b)). Exx.:

toxm morγ < *toxm-e-morγ* egg.
rāh āhan < *rāh-e āhan* railway.

§ **68.** Singular for Plural: The singular is used for the plural nouns
(a) to denote an indeterminate quantity. Exx.:

mehmān dāram I have guests.
bāγče por az gol būd The garden was full of flowers.

(b) in the predicate. Exx.:

se nafar az mosāferin xānom hastand (D) Three of the passengers are ladies.
dīšab hamegī mehmān-e doulat-e holand būdīm (D) Yesterday we were all of us guests of the Dutch government.
mosalmānān bāyad hame bā ham berādar bāšand Muslims must all be brothers to one another.

Note: On the use of the singular after numerals see § 78.

Adjectives

Use and omission of the *eẓāfe*.

§ 69. The attributive adjective normally follows the noun it qualifies and is joined to it by the *eẓāfe*. See § 14. Exx.:

āb-e garm hot water.
deraxt-e boland tall tree.
xāk-e siyāh black earth.

So too when the suffix *-ī* (the indefinite article, § 9), is attached to the end of the phrase:

ketāb-e bozorgī a large book
dast-e sefīdī a white hand.

If, however, the *-ī* is attached to the noun, the *eẓāfe* is omitted:

ketābī bozorg
dastī sefīd.

Note: In these latter cases the adjective is sometimes separated from the noun by the copulative verb. Exx.:

ʿemāratī ast bozorg It is a large building.
mouẓūʿī ast xeịlī ǰāleb-e tavaǰǰoh It is a very interesting subject.

§ 70. The *eẓāfe* is omitted

(a) when the adjective precedes the noun it qualifies. Exx.:

bad kārī karde ī You have done a bad thing.
xūb čīzī yādam dādī You have taught me a good thing.
ʿaǰab γalaṭī kardīm We have made a strange mistake.
bīčāre rafīqemān gūyā kamī nāxoš ast Our poor friend is perhaps a little unwell.

(b) in set phrases (§§ 59 (b) and 67, *Note*), especially in the colloquial language. Exx.:

tūt ferangī < *tūt-e ferangī* strawberry (*lit.* European mulberry).
sīb zamīnī < *sīb-e zamīnī* potato (*lit.* earth apple).
xedmat neẓāmī < *xedmat-e neẓāmī* military service.

§ 71. Agreement of gender: In set phrases an Arabic adjective qualifying a broken plural (§ 13 B.) takes the feminine ending *-e*. Exx.:

afkār-e ʿāmme (< *ʿāmm*) public opinion (*lit.* public thoughts)
vasāyeṭ-e naqlīye (< *naqlī*) means of transport
mamālek-e motamaddene (< *motamadden*) civilized countries.

Degrees of Comparison

§ **72.** Use of the Comparative: The Persian equivalent to English *than* is either

(a) the preposition *az* (§ 45), when the comparison is between two persons or objects. Exx.:

in pesar aẓ ān doxtar bolandtar ast This boy is taller than that girl.
pādšāh-e zanbūrhā-ye ʿasal az sāyerin dorošt-tar o xoš-andām-tar ast The queen bee is larger and more shapely than the rest.

or

(b) the conjunction *tā* (§§ 50 and 96), when the comparison is between two clauses. Exx.:

ū bīštar asb dārad tā man (dāram) He has more horses than I (have).

Note: There is usually no equivalent to the English "that of" etc. after a comparison. Exx.:

havā-ye hendūstān az īrān garmtar ast The climate of India is hotter than (that of) Persia.
sakane-ye tehrān az hame-ye šahrhā-ye īrān bīštar ast The population of Tehran is greater than (that of) all (the other) towns of Persia.

§ **73.** The compound pronoun *har če* (§ 23) is used with the comparative
(a) as the equivalent of the English "the —er ... the —er." Exx.:

har če zūdtar behtar The sooner the better.
har če bozorgtar šavīm γeẕā bīštar mī xvāhīm The larger we grow the more food we need.

(b) to express the idea of "the most possible". Exx.:

har če bozorgtar the greatest possible.
har če tamāmtar the completest possible.

§ **74.** Use of the Superlative: The superlative is used

(a) attributively, in which case it precedes the noun it defines. Exx.:

behtarin ketāb The best book.
bozorgtarin šāʿer-e īrān The greatest Persian poet.
motamavveltarin šaxṣ-e donyā The richest man in the world.

(b) in the predicate connected by the *eẓāfe* with a plural noun. Exx.:

zerāʿat behtarīn-e kārhāst Agriculture is the best of employments.
šotor morγ bozorgtarīn-e morγhāst The ostrich is the largest of birds.
baʿd az sar gardan bālātarīn-e andāmhā ast After the head the neck is the highest of the members.

It cannot be used absolutely in the predicate; the comparative is used in its place with *az hame* "than all." Exx.:

in doxtar kūčaktar az hame ast This girl is the youngest (*lit.* smaller than all).

Pronouns

§ 75. Personal Pronouns: The personal pronouns, as the subject of a sentence, are used only for purposes of emphasis and contrast; otherwise the subject is sufficiently indicated by the personal endings (§ 34). Exx.:

gerdū rā man dīde am va māl-e-man ast. It was I who saw the walnut and it is mine.
šomā dar xāne mī nešīnīd va kārhā-ye kūčak rā anǰam mīdehīd ammā man rāh-e-dūr mīravam va hīzom-kāšī mīkonam. You sit in the house and do the small jobs but I go on a long journey and fetch the wood.

Note: In the colloquial language the pronouns are used even when no emphasis is intended.

§ 76. Suffixed Pronouns: The suffixed pronouns, as has already been pointed out (§ 17), are used to express both the possessive (or genitive) and the dative and accusative cases. Exx.:

pedaraš yak zanī barā-yaš gereft His father took a wife for him.
alān bīrūnat miāvaram o mīxoramat (S) Now I will pull you out and eat you.
ʿaks-e čand nafar pesar o doxtar nešānam dād (D) He showed me a photograph of several boys and girls.

Note 1: The suffixed pronouns are used much more frequently in the spoken than in the literary language. Only in the former may they be attached to the simple prepositions (§ 45). Exx.:

yādaš āmad ke pedaraš beš sefāreš karde būd ke har vaqt rūzgār azat bar gašt bīl bedast begīr (S) He remembered (*lit.* there came the memory to him) that his father had told (*lit.* recommended to) him: "Whenever fortune is unfavourable to you (*lit.* turns away from you) take your spade in hand."

Note 2: On the use of the suffixed pronouns in place of *xod* etc. see § 77.

§ 77. The uses of *xod*: The pronoun *xod* is used

(a) as a reflexive pronoun like the English *myself*, *himself*, etc., in the colloquial language usually with the appropriate suffixed pronoun. If used with a noun or personal pronoun the latter either follows connected by the *eẓāfe* or (more rarely) precedes without the *eẓāfe*. Exx.:

xodešān raftand They went themselves.
zan xodaš rā košt The woman killed herself.
xod-e ān mard rā dīdam I saw that man himself.
man xod āmadam I came myself.

(b) as the equivalent of the English *own* (expressed or understood) preceded by the appropriate possessive pronoun. When referring back to the subject of the sentence it is in the literary language always substituted for the equivalent pronoun. Exx.:

asb-e xodaš rā beman forūxt He sold me his (own) horse.
ketāb-e xodam rā beū dādam. I gave him my book.
'aks-e xodetān rā beman nešān bedehīd Show me your photograph.

Note: In the colloquial language the suffixed pronouns may be used in such sentences without *xod.* Exx.:

xvāheš mī konam dastmālat rā beman bedeh ke dastam rā xošk bekonam Please give me your towel to dry my hands.
čamedānam rā dar qeṭār goẕāštam (D) I put my suitcase in the train.

Numerals

§ 78. Cardinals: Nouns following cardinals are in the singular number. Exx.:

do sāl two years
panǰ rūz five days
čehel sotūn forty pillars.

In the case of living beings and concrete things a classifier is normally inserted between the numeral and the noun. Of these classifiers the commonest are *nafar* "individual" for persons and *tā* "fold" for things. Exx.:

do nafar mohandes two engineers
čahār tā oṭāq four rooms

Other classifiers are:

bāb (door) for houses
tan (body) for persons
ǰeld (volume) for books
dāne (grain) for small round objects
ra's (head) for horses, cattle etc.
'adad (number) for small objects
farvand (helm) for ships
qabẓe (hilt) for swords and other weapons.

Exx.:

do ǰeld ketāb two books
se dāne sīb three apples
panǰāh ra's gūsfand fifty sheep
bīst farvand kaštī twenty ships
čahār qabẓe tofang four rifles

Note: In the colloquial language *tā* can be used for persons also. Exx.:
yūgandā čahār tā pādšāh dārad (D) Uganda has four kings.

The Verb

Indicative Mood

Tenses from the Present Stem

§ 79. Simple Present: The Simple Present (§ 35.1), normally replaced in the modern language by the Continuous Present (§§ 35.2 and 80), is used to express a general truth or describe a general action. Exx.:

besyār farq bāšad az ḥarf tā ʿamal There is a great deal of difference between speech (*lit.* word) and action.
herodot movarrex-e maʿrūf gūyad ke ṣad hazār kārgar moddat-e bīst sāl ānrā sāxtand (D) Herodotus, the celebrated historian, says that 100,000 workmen built it in a period of 20 years.

Note: dāštan "to have" admits only of the Simple Present (and Past) except in compound expressions.

§ 80. Continuous Present: The Continuous Present (§ 35.2) is used

(a) as in English, to describe an action still in progress. Exx.:

kār mīkonam I am working.
baččehā dar bāγ mīdavand The children are running in the garden.

Note: In the colloquial language this meaning is conveyed by the use of the Simple Present of *dāštan* in connection with the appropriate form of the Continuous Present. Exx.:

dāram mīravam I am going.
ḥālā dārīm az rū-ye baγdād mīgoẕarīm (D) We are now passing over Baghdad.

(b) to express a general truth. Exx.:

bīštar-e mardom-e ʿerāq bezabān-e ʿarabī soxan mīgūyand Most of the people of Iraq speak the Arabic language.
abrīšom az kerm-e abrīšom bedast mīāyad Silk is produced (lit. comes to hand) from the silkworm.

(c) to describe an habitual action. Exx.:

har rūz sāʿat-e panǰ o nīm boland mīšavam Every day I get up at half past five.
dar zamestān parastū az ǰāhā-ye sard begarmsīr mīravad va dar tābestān bar mī gardad In the winter the swallow goes from the cold places to the tropics and in the summer it returns.

(d) in the colloquial language (as in English) in place of the Future (§ 38). Exx.:

fardā betehrān mīāyam I am going to Tehran to-morrow.
ṣobḥ zūd haminke ṣadā-ye xorūs dar āmad man pā mīšavam mīravam (S) Early in the morning as soon as the cock crows (*lit.* the sound of the cock has come out) I shall get up and go.

Tenses from the Past Stem

§ 81. Simple Past: The Simple Past is used

(a) in narrative. Exx.:

gorg raft va ba'd az čand daqīqe bar gašt va dar zad (S) The wolf went away and after a few minutes returned and knocked on the door.
fardā ṣobḥ qīr āvord āb kard va rū-ye sang-e siyāh rīxt (S) The next day he brought some tar, melted it and poured it on the black stone.

(b) in present or future contexts, in temporal and conditional clauses, to indicate that the action precedes that described in the main clause. Exx.:

vaqtī ke da'vāmān šod marā bā či mīzanī (S) When we have a quarrel (*lit.* a quarrel became to us) what will you beat me with?
agar kasī āmad dar zad az darz-e dar o sūrax-e kelīdān xūb negāh konīd, agar man būdam vā konīd va agar gorg yā šayāl būd vā nakonīd (S) If someone comes and knocks on the door have a good look through the chink in the door and the keyhole; if it is I open [the door] and if it is the wolf or the jackal do not open [it].

(c) to describe an event that has just taken place. Exx.:

āteš gereft It has (just) caught fire.
āmadam mory o dīgam rā begīram (S) I have come to get my fowl and pot.

(d) to describe an event that is to take place immediately. Exx.:

raftam I am going (now at once)
to berou va man ham āmadam You go and I will come too.

§ 82. Continuous Past: The Continuous Past (§ 36.1) is used
(a) to describe an action as being still in progress. Exx.:

yak rūz gonješkī tū-ye biyābān mī parīd (S) One day a sparrow was flying in the desert.
rūzī nazdīk-e yorūb-e āftāb az xarābe-ī mī gozašt (S) One day just before sunset he was passing a ruin.

Note: In the colloquial language this meaning is conveyed by the use of the Simple Past of *dāštan* "to have" in connection with the appropriate form of the Continuous Past. Exx.:

dāšt mīraft He was going.
dāštam mīneveštam I was writing.

(b) to describe an habitual action. Exx.:

har sāl beīrān mīraftam I used to go to Persia every year.
har rūz ṣobḥ ke rūbāh az lāne-aš bīrūn miāmad negāhī bebālā-ye deraxt mī kard va salāmī be lak-lak mīdād va bā xodaš mīgoft ... (S) Every morning when the fox came out of its lair it would cast a glance up into the tree, utter a greeting to the stork and say to itself ...

(c) in conditional sentences, when the condition is impossible (§ 95 II).

(d) to express an unfulfilled wish. Exx.:

kāškī mīraft Would that he had gone.!
delam mīxvāst pā'in mīāmadam va pahlū-ye ān (rūdxāne) mīīstādam (D) I (*lit.* my heart) wished I could have come down and stood beside that (river).

Note: In the colloquial language the Continuous Past may be used instead of the Perfect Subjunctive after *bāyest* (§ 81 (b)). Exx.:

nabāyest in kār rā mīkardam I ought not to have done this thing.
man bāyest mīdānestam I ought to have known.

Tenses with the Past Participle

§ **83.** Perfect: The Perfect (§ 37.1) is used

(a) to describe an action or state in the past of which the effects continue into the present. Exx.:

hīč vaqt ūrā nadīde am I have never seen him.
xodā bešomā hūš dāde ast ke hame čīz rā betavānīd befahmīd God has given you intelligence in order that you may be able to understand everything.
az kaštī-hā'ī ke tā beḥāl az mā gozašte and bīštar kaštī-hā-ye nāft-kaš va aylab yā ītāliyā'ī yā ferānsavī būde and (D) Of the ships which have passed us up till now most have been oil-tankers and for the greater part French or Italian.
alān māh nūr-e xod rā dar jelou-e mā rū-ye kānāl paxš karde va manẓare-ye besyār jālebī ījād karde ast (D) Now the moon has scattered its light in front of us on the Canal and produced a very attractive scene.

(b) in making statements (as distinct from narration) about events or conditions in the past. In such contexts the Continuous Perfect (§ 37.2) performs the function of the Continuous Past. Exx.:

pedarān-e mā dar īrān zendegī karde and Our forefathers lived in Persia.
eskandar az pādšāhān-e bozorg-e yūnān-e qadīm būde ast Alexander was [one] of the great kings of ancient Greece.
ḥakīm 'omar-e xaiyām ke az dānešmandān o šo'arā-ye bozorg-e īrān būde dar 'aṣr-e malekšāh mīzīste ast The philosopher Omar Khayyam, who was one of the great scholars and poets of Persia, lived in the age of Malik-Shah.

(c) as a kind of *oratio obliqua* indicating that the facts are not given on the authority of the narrator. Here too the Continuous Perfect replaces the Continuous Past. Exx.:

mouqe'ī ke dar xedmat-e neẓām būde va be nafarāt-e xod dars-e nāranjakandāzī mīdāde ast nāranjak dar-rafte va dastaš rā ma'yūb karde

va baʿd ānrā boride and (D) When he was in the army (*lit.* military service) and was giving his men instruction in grenade-throwing the grenade went off and damaged his hand, and afterwards they amputated it.
kāγaẕī az pedaraš āmad bein maẓmūn ke pesaraš yaʿnī rafīq-e man az jang bāz nagašte va az qarār-e maʿlūm bedast-e žāponīhā oftāde va dar kaštī ke beasīrī mīrafte marīẓ būde va baʿdan ān kaštī γarq šode va aγlab az ānhā ke dar kaštī būde and γarq šode and (D) A letter came from his father to the effect that his son, i.e. my friend, had not returned from the war. Apparently he had fallen into the hands of the Japanese and had been ill in the ship in which he was going into captivity. Afterwards that ship had been sunk and most of those that were on board had been drowned.

(d) to express our Future Perfect in sentences of the type of sentence listed under § 96 (e).

§ 84. Pluperfect: The Pluperfect (§ 37.4) is used

(a) to describe a past event that preceded another past event. Exx.:
yak šab šāmaš rā xorde būd ke dīd bād-e sardī mīāyad (S) One night she had eaten her supper when she noticed (*lit.* saw) that a cold wind was blowing (*lit.* is coming).
yak rūz mehrak be biyābān rafte būd; čašmaš be xarman-hā oftād (S) One day Mehrak had gone into the open country; his eye fell upon the crops.
rūbāh hamān ḥarfhā'ī ke be xorūs zade būd begorg zad (S) The fox spoke (*lit.* struck) the same words to the wolf as he had spoken to the cock.

(b) in conditional sentences relating to the past when the condition is impossible (§ 95 II (b)).

Subjunctive Mood

§ 85. Present Subjunctive: The Present Subjunctive (§ 34.3) is used in subordinate clauses, whether the verb of the main sentence is in the present or the past,

(a) in reference to a present or future event or condition about which there is some doubt. Exx.:
alān gamān mīkonam [ke] bar rū-ye rūd-xāne-ye qare sū bāšīm (D) I think we are now over the River Qara Su.
mītarsam [ke] šīrī babrī yā jānvarī darande biyāyad va marā bexorad (S) I am afraid a lion, tiger or [other] ravenous animal will come and eat me.

Note: The conjunction *ke* "that" is usually omitted.

(b) as the equivalent of the English infinitive governed by a verb. In these cases the conjunction *ke* "that" is normally omitted. Exx.:

mīxvāham beīrān beravam I wish to go (*lit.* I may go) to Persia.
natavānest zūdtar biyāyad He was unable to come (*lit.* he may come) earlier.
taṣmīm gereft taḥṣīl konad He decided to study (*lit.* he may study).
sa'y xvāham kard nāme benevīsam I shall try to write (*lit.* I may write) a letter.

(c) after the Simple Present of the impersonal verbs *bāyestan* "to be necessary" and *šāyestan* "to be possible" (§ 44) reference to the present or future. (On the use of the Short Infinitive after these verbs see § 89). In these cases *ke* is always omitted in the modern language. Exx.:

bāyad beorūpā beravam I must go (*lit.* It is necessary I go) to Europe.
nabāyad injā bemānīd You must not remain (*lit.* It is not necessary you remain) here.
šāyad fardā biyāyad Perhaps (*lit.* It is possible) he will come to-morrow.

Note 1: gūyā "perhaps" (§ 48 (4)) also takes the subjunctive.

Note 2: šāyad and *gūyā* may also be followed by the indicative.

(d) in general relative clauses. Exx.:

har kas šarāb bexorad šeiṭān mīšavad Whoever drinks wine becomes a devil.
oṣūlan har jā āb bāšad zībā'ī yāft mīšavad (D) In general wherever there is water beauty is to be found.

(e) in the protasis of conditional sentences relating to the future (§ 95 I (a)).

(f) after *tā* and *ke* in final and certain other senses (§§ 96 and 97).

(g) after the conjunctive phrases (§ 51 (b)) *bejā-ye inke* and *dar 'avaż-e* "instead of (this that)," *bedūn-e inke* "without (this that), unless," *pīš az ānke* and *qabl az ānke* "before" and *joz īnke* and *γeir az īnke* "except (this that)." Exx.:

mā dar 'avaż-e inke nazdīkhā-ye landan bāšīm hanūz dar jazīre-ye mālt mībāšīm (D) Instead of being near London we are still on the island of Malta.
pīš az inke in kāγaz rā šorū' konam yak enšā' barā-ye fardā neveštam (D) Before I began (*lit.* may begin) this letter I wrote an essay for to-morrow.

Note: In the case of verbal expressions (§ 60) the prefix *be-* is usually omitted so that the verbal form is identical with the corresponding form of the Simple Present (§ 35.1). In the case of *dāštan* "to have," which admits only of the Simple Present, the Perfect Subjunctive is substituted for the Present. See § 87 (d).

§ 86. Present Subjunctive: The Present Subjunctive is used in main sentences

(a) to supply the 1st and 3rd persons of the Imperative (§ 35.4). Exx.:

beravīm let us go.
biyāyad let him come.
bebīnam let me see.

(b) as an Optative. Exx.:

xodā ūrā biyāmorzad May God forgive him!
sāye-ye šomā kam našavad May your shadow not become less!

Note: On the isolated optative form *bād* "may ... be" see § 41.3 *Note.*

(c) in expressing doubt as to a future action. Exx.:

čekār bekonam kojā beravam What am I to do? Where shall I go?

§ 87. Perfect Subjunctive: The Perfect Subjunctive is used

(a) in reference to a past event or condition about which there is some doubt. Exx.:

mītarsam ū rafte bāšad I fear he has gone.
omīdvāram har do kāγaẕ rasīde bāšad I hope (*lit.* am hopeful) both letters have arrived.

(b) After the Simple Present and Simple Past of *bāyestan* "to be necessary" and the Simple Present of *šāyestan* "to be possible" in reference to the past. Exx.:

bāyad rafte bāšad He must have gone (*lit.* It is necessary he may have gone.)
nabāyest in kār rā karde bāšīd You ought not to have done (*lit.* It was not necessary you may have done) this thing.
šāyad in rā nadāneste bāšand Perhaps (*lit.* It is possible) they may not have known this.

(c) in the protasis of conditional sentences relating to the past (§ 95 I (b)).

(d) in the case of *dāštan* "to have" in place of the Present Subjunctive. Exx.:

bāyad asb dāšte bāšam I must have a horse.
xeịlī pīš az inke englīs-hā šāh dāšte bāšand mā šāh dāštīm (D) We had kings long before the British had.

§ 88. The Infinitive: The Infinitive (§ 36) cannot as in English be directly governed by a personal verb, its place being in such cases taken by a verb in the Present Subjunctive (§ 85 (b)). Its function is that of a gerund or verbal noun, the subject or object being linked to it by means of the *eẕāfe*. Exx.:

pas az āšāmīdan-e āb labhāyam rā bā dastmāl pāk mīkonam After drinking water I wipe my lips with a towel.

hangām-e nafas kašīdan dahānam rā mī bandam When breathing (*lit.* [at] the time of breathing) I close my mouth.
kār-e xūn rasānīdan-e γeẕā be hame-ye badan ast The function of the blood is to send (*lit.* the sending of) food to the whole of the body.
hanūz xvāndan rā namīdānam I still do not know how to read (*lit.* reading).
az mordan xalāṣ šodam I was saved from dying.

Note: An indefinite noun may precede the infinitive, as is always the case with nominal phrases (§ 60 (b)). Exx.:

hangām-e γeẕā xordan āranǰam rā rū-ye mīz namīgoẕāram When eating food I do not put my elbows on the table.
hīzom šekastan bīl zadan naǰǰārī kardan hame-ye inhā varzesh ast Chopping (*lit.* breaking) wood, using (*lit.* striking) a spade and doing carpentry — all these things are exercise.

§ 89. Short Infinitive: The Short Infinitive (§ 36) is used

(a) with the Simple Present of *xvāstan* to form the Future (§ 38).

(b) After impersonal verbs (§ 44) and phrases when the agent is not named. Exx.:

bāyad raft One must go (*lit.* It is necessary to go).
gāhī bāyad darhā rā bāz kard tā havā-ye xūb dāxel bešavad Sometimes one must (*lit.* it is necessary to) open the doors so that the good air may come in (*lit.* become entering).
benā bar natāyeǰī ke tā konūn bedast āmade namītavān yak ʿaqīde-ye qaṭʿī ḥāsel kard valī behame ḥāl mītavān goft ke entexāb-konandegān-e ferānse bīštar motamāyel beḥezb-e sosiyālist mī bāšand From (*lit.* according to) the results that have so far come to hand it is impossible to form (*lit.* obtain) a definite opinion but in any case it can be said (*lit.* it is possible to say) that the electors of France are inclined towards the Socialist Party.

§ 90. Participles: The Present Participle in *-ande* (§ 35) is used

(a) as a *nomen actoris*. Exx.:

nevīsande writer
xvānande reader
entexāb-konande elector

(b) as an attributive adjective. Exx.:

hafte-ye āyande next (*lit.* coming) week.
zahr-e košande deadly (*lit.* killing) poison.
ǰānvar-e darande fierce (*lit.* tearing) animal.

§ 91. The Present Participle in *-ān* (§ 35) is used

(a) as a gerund, often reduplicated. Ex.:

davān davān āmad He came running.

(b) as an adjective, attributive or predicative. Exx.:

bād-e sūzān burning wind
pesarhā šād o xandān būdand The boys were happy and smiling.

§ **92.** The Future Participle formed by adding *-ī* to the infinitive (§ 36) is used like the Latin gerundive. Exx.:

in xordanī nīst This is not to be eaten.
čīzhā-ye goftanī xei̯lī ziyād ast (D) There are very many things to be said (*lit.* The things to be said are very many).

§ **93.** The Past Participle (§ 36) can be either active or passive.

I. It is used actively

(a) in conjunction with the verb *būdan* "to be" to form the compound tenses of the verb (§ 37).

(b) as a gerund. Exx.:

xarī pūst-e šīrī pei̯dā karde pūšīd A donkey having found a lion's skin put [it] on.
bāγbān sabadī por az mīve karde bešahr āvord The gardener having filled (*lit.* made full) a basket with fruit brought [it] to town.
xedmatkār dar-e otāqrā nabaste pei̯-e xedmat raft The servant went about his duties (*lit.* after service) without (*lit.* not) having shut the door of the room.

In the above examples the gerund refers to an action prior to that expressed by the main verb. It may also be used, in co-ordinated sentences, as a substitute for each finite verb except the last, the clauses usually being linked with the conjunction *va* "and". Exx.:

ītāliya dar ǰonūb-e orūpā vāqeʿ šode (= *vāqeʿ ast*) *va pāyetaxt-e ān rom ast* Italy lies in the south of Europe and its capital is Rome.
pāreʾ ī az qārčhā zahrnāk būde (= *ast*) *va čun tamīz-e ānhā bā qārčhā-ye xorākī došvār ast bīštar bexoṣūṣ dar faṣl-e bahār o tābestān mardom az nādānī ānhā rā xorde* (= *mīxorand*) *va masmūm mīšavand* Some (*lit.* a piece of) mushrooms are poisonous and since it is difficult to distinguish them (*lit.* the distinction of them is difficult) from (*lit.* with) edible mushrooms people often eat them out of ignorance and are poisoned, especially in the seasons of spring and summer.

II. It is used passively

(a) in conjunction with *šodan* "to become" to form the passive tenses of the verb (§ 39).

(b) as an adjective. Exx.:

nān-e sūxte burnt bread
āb-e ǰūšīde boiled water
gūšt-e poxte cooked meat.

Note 1: It can also be used as a noun and take a plural ending. Exx.:

koštegān the killed < *košte* killed.
gomāštegān delegates, servants < *gomāšte* delegated.
bāz-dāštegān detainees < *bāz-dāšte* detained.

Note 2: It can be used in similar fashion in the case of intransitive verbs also. Exx.:

sāl-e gozašte last (*lit.* the past) year.
mordegān the dead < *morde* dead.

Note also *īstāda* "standing" as well as "(having) stood," *nešaste* "sitting" as well as "(having) sat."

§ **94.** Conjunctions: Of the remaining parts of speech only certain of the Conjunctions (§ 50) present syntactical problems: *agar* "if," because of its use in conditional sentences; *tā* "until, in order that, so long as," which takes the indicative or the subjunctive according to the meaning; and *ke* "that," which, in addition to its functions as a conjunction, also does service as a kind of relative pronoun.

Note: On the use of the subjunctive after certain conjunctive phrases see § 85 (g).

§ **95.** agar: *agar* introduces the protasis of conditional sentences, which may be divided into two classes, according as the condition is possible or impossible.

I. Possible Conditions

(a) When relating to the present or future these take the Present Subjunctive in the protasis and the Continuous Present or Future in the apodosis. Exx.:

agar fardā biyāyam berādaram ham xvāhad āmad If I come tomorrow my brother will come too.
agar badan-e ensān rā bederaxt tašbīh konīm dast o pā-hā bemanẕele-ye šāxe-hā-ye deraxt xvāhad būd If we compare the human body (*lit.* body of man) to a tree the hands and feet will be like (*lit.* in the rank of) the branches of the tree.
agar marā bekošī bačče-hā-ye man bī mādar mī mānand va torā nafrin mī konand (S) If you kill me my young ones will be left motherless and will curse you.

Note 1: In sentences of this type *čonanče* (§ 51 (a), *Note*) may be substituted for *agar*.

Note 2: When the action described in the protasis precedes that described in the apodosis, the Simple Past is usually substituted for the Subjunctive. See § 81 (b). In sentences of this type *har gāh* (§ 51 (a), *Note*) may be substituted for *agar*.

Note 3: When there is no element of doubt the Continuous Present may be substituted for the Subjunctive. Exx.:

agar mīxvāhī hame-ye rū-ye zamin rā bebīnī bāyad ham asb o ham kaštī dāšte bāšī If you wish to see the whole surface of the earth you must have both a horse and a ship.

(b) When the action described in the protasis is in the past the verb is in the Perfect Subjunctive. Exx.:

agar nāme-ye ūrā xvānde bāšīd mī dānīd koǰā rafte ast If you have read his letter you know where he has gone.

agar in ketāb rā nadīde bāšīd bešomā nešān mīdeham If you have not seen this book I will show it to you.

agar ḥasan rafte bāšad in pūl rā beberādaraš bedehīd If Hasan has gone give this money to his brother.

Note: When no doubt is expressed the Perfect Indicative may be substituted for the Subjunctive. Ex.:

agar šanīde īd pas dāstānaš ham bešenavīd (S) If you have heard (the saying) then hear the story of it also.

II. Impossible Conditions

(a) When relating to the present these take the Continuous Past in both the protasis and the apodosis. Exx.:

agar ūrā mīdīdam namīšenaxtam If I saw him I should not know him.

agar mīdānestam namīporsīdam If I knew I should not ask.

agar beman eǰāze mīdādand mīraftam If they allowed me I should go.

Note: Since *būdan* "to be" and *dāštan* "to have" do not normally allow of the Continuous Past (§§ 42 and 79 Note) the Simple Past is usually substituted in the case of these verbs but the Continuous Past is also possible. Exx.:

agar pīr būdam namīraftam If I were old I should not go.

agar rūd-e nīl namībūd hīčkas dar meṣr namītavānest zendegī bekonad If it were not for the River Nile (*lit.* If the River Nile were not) no one could live in Egypt.

agar zūr dāštam āftāb ābam namīkard (S) If I were strong (*lit.* had strength) the sun would not melt me.

agar man zūr mīdāštam ʿalaf saram sabz namīšod (S) If I were strong (*lit.* had strength) grass would not grow (*lit.* become green) on me.

(b) When relating to the past they may either take the Continuous Past in both clauses or else substitute the Pluperfect in the protasis, the apodosis or both. Exx.:

agar zūdtar mīraftand sar-e vaqt mīrasīdand If they had gone earlier they would have arrived in time.

agar ūrā dīde būdam namīšenāxtam If I had seen him I should not have known him.

agar gerān nabūd xarīde būdam If it had not been dear I should have bought it.

§ 96. **tā**: *tā* is employed in a number of different meanings:

(a) "until." In this sense it takes the Present Subjunctive in present or future contexts and the Simple Past when referring to an actual event in the past. Exx.:

ṣabr konīd tā biyāyad Wait (*lit.* make patience) until he comes.
mogholān az pei̯-e ū mīšetāftand tā ʿāqebat be jazīre'ī az daryā-ye māzandarān panāh bord The Mongols hurried after him until in the end he took refuge on an island in the Caspian Sea (*lit.* Sea of Mazandaran).

Note: In sentences referring to future time in which the verb in the main clause is in the negative the clause introduced by *tā* (which in these cases always precedes the main clause) is also in the negative. Exx.:

tā beman ejāze nadehīd beū namīgūyam I shall not tell him until you give me permission.
tā ānrā bečašm-e xodam nabīnam bāvar namīkonam I shall not believe until I see it with my own eyes.

Note 2: When referring to past events *tā* may be replaced by the conjunctional phrases *tā īnke* "until this that," *tā ānke* "until that that," *tā vaqtīke, tā mou̯qeʿīke* "until the time that." Ex.:

sorx-pūstān dar jangalhā o kanār-e rūdxāne-hā zendegī mīkardand va hamīše bā ham dar zad o xord būdand tā ānke sefīd-pūstān beemrīkā raftand va dar ānjā šahrhā-ye bozorg sāxtand The redskins lived in the forests and along the rivers and were always in conflict with one another until the whiteskins went to America and built great cities there.

(b) "in order that." In this sense it always takes the Present Subjunctive. Exx.:

ketābrā beū dādam tā bexvānad I gave him the book to read (*lit.* in order that he may read).
bešahr raftam tā berādar-e ūrā bebīnam I went to the town to see (*lit.* in order that I may see) his brother.

Note 3: Cf. the use of *ke* (§§ 85 (f) and 97 (b)) in the same sense.

(c) "as long as." In this sense it takes the Indicative. Ex.:

tā pedaram īnjā mīmānad man ham bāyad bemānam As long as my father remains here I too must remain.

(d) "as soon as," with the Simple Past, whether referring to the past or the future. Cf. §§ 81 (b) and 95 I (a) Note 2. Exx.:

tā marā dīd ferār kard As soon as he saw me he ran away.
tā bešahr rasīdīd bemanzel-e ḥasan beravīd As soon as you arrive in the town go to Hasan's house.

(e) "by the time that," with the Present Subjunctive in relation to the future and the Simple Past when relating to an event in the past. Exx.:

tā bemanzel-e šomā berasam dīr xvāhad šod By the time I reach your house it will be late.
tā ū ḥarakat konad man rafte am By the time he sets out I shall have gone.
tā pežeshk āmad berādaram bīhūš šode būd By the time the doctor came my brother had lost consciousness (*lit.* become unconscious).

Note 4: On *tā* in the sense of "than" see § 72 (b).

§ **97.** ke: As a conjunction *ke* is used

(a) to introduce clauses dependent on verbs of saying, thinking, knowing, seeing, etc. In thus reproducing speech or thought the Persian practice is either to retain the forms of direct speech or else simply to change the first person, when necessary, to the third, whilst leaving the tense unaltered. Note that in sentences of this type *ke* may be readily omitted. Exx.:
goft ke fardā miāyam He said that he was coming (*lit.* I am coming) to-morrow.
goft ke fardā miāyad He said that he was coming (*lit.* is coming) to-morrow.
xar fahmīd ke īn šīr ast (S) The donkey realized that this was (*lit.* is) a lion.
dīd [ke] do bačče dar ḥayāṭ rāh mīravand He saw that two children were (*lit.* are) walking about in the courtyard.
dīd [ke] kešāvarzī dārad zamin rā bīl mīzanad (S) He saw that a cultivator was (*lit.* is) breaking the ground with his spade.

(b) to introduce final clauses. See § 85 (f) In such sentences also the conjunction is often omitted. Exx.:
kafgīr rā gereft ke dīg rā beham bezanad (S) He took the ladle in order to (*lit.* that he may) stir the pot.
raft pahlū-ye kadxodā ke moryaš rā begīrad (S) He went to the headman to (*lit.* that he may) fetch his fowl.
āmadam [ke] mory o dīgam rā begīram (S) I have come to (*lit.* that I may) fetch my fowl and my pot.

(c) in the sense of "because." Ex.:
berou̯ bīrūn ke ṣobḥ šod (S) Go out because it is (*lit.* has become) morning.

(d) in the sense of "when," the conjunction being placed after the first word or phrase of the subordinate clause, which in such cases precedes the main clause. Exx.:
tābestān ke gozašt pā'īz miāyad When summer has passed autumn comes.
qadrī ke gardeš kardand xersī az dūr pei̯da šod When they had walked a little (way) a bear appeared in the distance.
ṣadāš ke begūš-e xar rasīd nazdīk būd ke zahre tark bešavad (S) When his voice reached the donkey's ears his gall-bladder nearly burst (*lit.* it was near that his gall-bladder may burst).

Note 1: In sentences of a different kind in which the temporal clause follows a main clause with the verb in the Continuous Past or Pluperfect and has its own verb in the Simple Past, the temporal clause is introduced by *ke*. Ex.:

hanūz čašm beham nagozāšte būd ke dīd ṣadā-ye dar mī āyad (S) She had not yet closed her eyes when she heard (*lit.* saw) there was a knock at the door (*lit.* the sound of the door is coming).

(e) as a kind of expletive after the first word or phrase of the sentence. This is very common in the spoken language, often serving to convey a note of protest. Exx.:

mā ham ke ṣadā'ī dārīm (S) I (*lit.* we) have a voice too, you know.
a'ṣāb ke fūlād nīst (D) [One's] nerves are not [made of] steel, you know.

§ 98. As a relative particle *ke* is used in conjunction with the appropriate personal pronoun expressed or understood within the relative clause. When this latter is restrictive the antecedent takes the relative suffix -*ī* (§ 23), not to be confused with the Indefinite Article (§ 9 (a)). The personal pronoun is normally omitted when it would be in the nominative or accusative. Exx.:

γezā'ī ke mīxorīm vāred-e xūn mīšavad The food that we eat enters the blood.
in heivān ke šaklaš rā mī bīnīd esmaš vazaγ ast This animal whose picture you see (*lit.* that you see its picture) is called a frog.
zarde ke rangaš zard ast dar vasaṭ-e sefīde ast The yolk, the colour of which (*lit.* that its colour) is yellow, is in the middle of the white.
āmūzgār ẓarfī az šīše āvord ke māhī dar ān būd The teacher brought a glass bowl in which there was a fish (*lit.* that there was a fish in it).
zabān 'ozvī gūštin ast ke behar ṭaraf ḥarakat mī konad va bā ān soxan mī gū'īm The tongue is a fleshy member which moves in every direction and with which we speak (*lit.* we speak with it).

Note 1: When the unexpressed pronoun in the relative clause would have been in the accusative, the particle *rā* (§§ 11 (a) and 64) may be attached to the antecedent, if this is the subject of the sentence. Ex.:

xānvāde'ī rā ke mīšenāsam bā do bačče dar šahrī dar nazdīkī-ye kemberīj maskan dārand (D) A family that I know live with their two children in a town near Cambridge.

Note 2: ke is often added to *ānče* (§ 23), especially when it is followed by *rā*. Ex.:

ānče rā ke dīdīm besyār zībā ast (D) What we saw is very beautiful.

Bibliography

A. Grammar

A. Bausani, *Di una possibile origine dell' accentuazione sull' ultima sillaba in persiano moderno, Oriente Moderno* 27 (1947) pp. 122–130.

J. A. Boyle, *The changes of meaning undergone by certain Persian nomina agentis in -tār (-dār), Journal of the Royal Asiatic Society*, 1952, pp. 13–23.

—, *Notes on the colloquial language of Persia as recorded in certain recent writings, Bulletin of the School of Oriental and African Studies* 14 (1952), pp. 451–462.

L. P. Elwell-Sutton, *Elementary Persian grammar*, Cambridge 1963.

E. M. N. Hawker, *Written and spoken Persian*, 3rd ed., London 1957.

W. Hinz, *Persisch I*, Berlin 1942.

A. K. S. Lambton, *Persian grammar*, Cambridge 1953.

G. Lazard, *Grammaire du persan contemporain*, Paris 1957.

W. Lentz, *Neupersisch* in *Handbuch der Orientalistik, I, Linguistik*, Leiden 1958.

M. Minovi, *A note on Persian grammar: plural subjects and singular verbs, Journal of the Royal Asiatic Society*, 1942, pp. 41–47.

L. S. Peisikov, *Tegeranskiį dialekt*, Moscow 1960.

—, *Voprosī sintaksisa persidskogo yazīka*, Moscow 1959.

D. C. Phillott, *Higher Persian grammar*, Calcutta 1919.

Mansour Shaki, *Nominal compounds in Neo-Persian, Archiv Orientální* 31 (1963) pp. 138–140.

S. Telegdi, *Beiträge zur historischen Grammatik des Neupersischen, I, Acta Orientalia (Academia Scientiarum Hungarica)* 5 (1955), pp. 67–183.

—, *Nature et fonction des périphrases verbales dites 'verbes composés' en persan, ibid.* 1 (1950–51), pp. 315–338.

B. Lexicography

J. A. Boyle, *A practical dictionary of the Persian language*, London 1949.

W. Eilers, *Deutsch-persisches Wörterbuch*, Wiesbaden 1959ff.

S. Haïm, *Larger English-Persian dictionary*, 2 vols., Tehran 1941–43.

—, *New English Persian-English dictionary*, 2 vols., Tehran 1934–36.

—, *Shorter English-Persian dictionary*, Tehran 1953.

—, *Shorter Persian-English dictionary*, Tehran 1954.

A. K. S. Lambton, *Persian vocabulary*, Cambridge 1954.

B. V. Miller, *Persidsko-russkiį slovar'*, Moscow 1950.

Y. Raḥmatī, *Farhang-e ʿāmiyāne, Amṣāl, loyāt o moṣtaleḥāt*, Tehran 1330/1951.

E. D. Ross, *Modern Persian colloquial, Bulletin of the School of Oriental Studies* 6 (1930–32), pp. 601–615.

C. Chrestomathies etc.

Iraǰ Afšar, *Naṣr-e fārsī-ye moʿāṣer*, Tehran 1330/1951.

A. J. Arberry, *Modern Persian reader*, Cambridge 1944.

R. Gelpke, *Modern Persian texts: selection, introduction and glossary*, Wiesbaden 1962.

MAHDĪ ḤAMĪDĪ. *Daryā-ye gouhar* I, Tehran, 2nd ed., 1334/1955.
H. D. G. LAW, *Persian Letters. A manual for students of Persian with introduction, translation, key, notes, and vocabulary*, London (1948).
V. MONTEIL, *Le persan contemporain. Textes et vocabulaire*, Paris 1955.
SA'ĪD NAFĪSĪ, *Šāhkārhā-ye naṣr-e fārsī-ye mo'āṣer*, Tehran 1330/1951.

D. Literature

(a) Literary history and criticism

A. J. ARBERRY, and H. D. G. LAW, *Persian writers, Life and Letters*, December 1949.
P. W. AVERY, *Developments in modern Persian prose, Muslim World* 45 (1955), pp. 313–323.
A. BAUSANI, *Notizie su poeti persiani contemporanei, Oriente Moderno* 25 (1945), pp. 28–41.
M. BORECKÝ, *Persian prose since* 1946, *Middle East Journal* 7 (1953), pp. 235–244.
[J. A. BOYLE], *Persian literature to-day, Times Literary Supplement*, June 12th 1953.
VĚRA KUBÍČKOVÁ, *Die neupersische Literatur des* 20. *Jahrhunderts* in JAN RYPKA, *Iranische Literaturgeschichte*, Leipzig 1959.
R. LESCOT, *Le roman et la nouvelle dans la littérature persane contemporaine, Bulletin d'Études Orientales* 9 (1942), pp. 83–101.
F. MACHALSKI, *Historyczna powieść perska*, Cracow 1952.
V. MONTEIL, *Un écrivain persan du demi-siècle: Sâdeq Hedâyat*, Tehran 1952.
B. NIKITINE, *Seyyed Mohammad Ali Djemalzadeh, Revue des Études Islamiques*, Paris 1959.
—, *Les thèmes sociaux dans la littérature persane moderne, Oriente Moderno* 34 (1954), pp. 225–237.
G. M. WICKENS, *Bozorg Alavi's Portmanteau, University of Toronto Quarterly* 28 (1959), pp. 116–133.
—, *Poetry in modern Persia, ibid.* 29 (1960), pp. 262–281.
E. YARSHATER, *Persian letters in the last fifty years, Middle Eastern Affairs* 9 (1960), pp. 262–281.
R. YASSEMI, *La poésie iranienne contemporaine* in *L'âme de l'Iran*, Paris 1951.

(b) Translations into European languages

BOZORG 'ALAVĪ, *Ihre Augen*, transl. H. Melzig, Berlin 1959.
—, See also Arberry and Law under (a).
ṢĀDEQ ČŪBAK, *The baboon whose buffoon was dead*, transl. P. W. Avery, *New World Writing* 11 (1957).
R. GELPKE, (transl.) *Persische Meistererzähler der Gegenwart*, Zürich 1960.
ṢĀDEQ HEDĀYAT, *The blind owl*, transl. D. P. Costello, London 1957.
—, *La chouette aveugle*, transl. R. Lescot, Paris 1953.
—, *Deux nouvelles*, ed. and transl. V. Monteil, Tehran 1952.
—, *Die Legende von der Schöpfung*, transl. M. Lorenz, Berlin 1960.
—, See also Gelpke above and Arberry and Law under (a).
MOḤAMMAD 'ALĪ ǦAMĀLZĀDE, *Choix de nouvelles*, trans. S. Corbin and E. Lotfi, Paris 1959.
—, See also Gelpke above.

Chrestomathy

I

آهـــو

آهو حیوان قشنگ صحرائی است. بعضی از آهوها شاخ کوتاه دارنـد، بعضی شاخ بلند. آهو دمش کوتاه، زیر شکمش سفید است وچشمهایش سیاه[1]. دست و پای آهو نازکست وخوب میتواند بدود. بچهٔ آهو را میگیرند، درخانه ها نگاه میدارند. کم کم انس میگیرد ودیگر فرار نمیکند.

اســب

اسب حیوان نجیب قشنگی است. گردن اسب موهای بلند دارد که آنرا یال میگویند. پاهای اسب سم دارد. اسب شیهه میکشد. بچهٔ اسب را کره میگویند. اسب سواری میدهد. گاری ودرشکه میکشد، بار هم میبرد ولی اسب سواری با اسب بارکش فرق دارد. اسب بارکش یابو است.

فیـــل

فیل حیوان بزرگیست. دو دندان دراز دارد. میان دو دندان فیل خرطوم بلندیست که بینی او است. ما هرچه میخواهیم بخوریم با دست بر میداریم وبدهان میگذاریم. فیل با خرطوم بر میدارد وبدهان میگذارد. پشت فیل تخت میگذارند وبر آن سوار میشوند. وطن فیل هندوستان است.

گاو نر، گاو ماده

گاو نر حیوان پر زوریست. زمین را شخم میکند وگاهی بار میبرد. گاو ماده شیر میدهد. از شیر کره، روغن، ماست، پنیر میسازند.

گوسفنـد

میش گوسفندیست که شاخ ندارد. قوچ گوسفندیست که شاخهای پیچیده دارد. بره بچهٔ گوسفند است. بره ها در صحرا دنبال مادرشان میدوند

[1]) § 61, *Note 2*.

و بع بع میکنند. گوسفند بما پشم میدهد. از آن پشم جوراب و پیراهن و پارچه های پشمی درست میکنند. از شیر گوسفند ماست وکره و روغن وپنیر وسرشیر میسازند.

زنبور عسل

این پرندهٔ کوچک زرد وسیاه که دو بال زیبا وچهار پا ودو دست دارد زنبور عسل است. زنبورهای عسل با یکدیگر زندگانی میکنند. پادشاه دارند پادشاه آنها از سایرین درشت تر وخوش اندام تر است. در برابر دشمن مانند سرباز صف میکشند، جنگ میکنند. زنبور عسل در بهار وتابستان صبح زود میرود، بر گلها می نشیند، شیرینی گل را مکیده میآورد ودر لانهٔ خود جمع میکند. ما آن شیرینی خوشمزه خوشبورا که اسمش عسلست از خانهٔ زنبور میگیریم واز خوردنش لذت میبریم. زنبور عسل از روی گل وگیاه چربی زرد رنگی میگیرد که اسمش موم است. موم بپای زنبور میچسبد، زنبور موم را میآورد بخانه ولانه های شش گوشه قشنگ ومحکم میسازد.

کرم ابریشم

این حیوان که بال وپر درآورده وپروانه شده است یک روزکرم کوچکی بوده واز لعاب دهنش تار ابریشم میساخته[1]. خوراک کرم ابریشم برگ توت است وبا لعاب دهان تار ورشتهٔ نازک ولطیف بیرون میدهد وکم کم دور خودش می تنند وخانه میسازد. آن خانه را پیله میگویند. هرکس آنرا ببیند[2] گمان میکند حیوانک میان پیله مرده است، اما نمرده بلکه در خواب است. کم کم پر وبال بیرون میآورد. همینکه پر وبالش درآمد واز خواب بیدار شد[3] هرگاه اورا با حرارت نکشند پیله را سوراخ میکند و بیرون میپرد. از ابریشم پارچه های حریر میبافند، از آن پارچه ها لباسهای قشنگ میدوزند. در مملکت ما کرم ابریشم خوب تربیت میشود. در رشت بهتر وبیشتر از هر جای ایران ابریشم بعمل میآید.

1) § 37. 2, *Note*, and 83 (b). — 2) § 85 (d). — 3) § 81 (b).

تابستـان

هوا در تابستان گرم میشود. روزها دراز و شبها کوتاه است[1]. آفتاب میوه هارا زود میرساند وشیرین میکند، گندم وجو در صحرا زرد میشود. برزگران گندم را اول دروکرده خرمن میکنند، بعد میکوبند وکاه آنرا ازگندم جدا کرده کاه را برای آذوقهٔ زمستانی حیوانات بانبار میبرند. گندم را بآسیا برده آرد میسازند. جورا هم باسب وخر میدهند. مورچه ها در تابستان دانه جمع میکنند تا در زمستان آسوده باشند. سعدی میفرماید.

مور گرد آورد در تابستان تا فراغت بود[2] زمستانش.

تابستان فصل خوبی است. بیشتر خوراک انسان وحیوان در این فصل آماده میشود.

پائیـز

تابستان که[3] گذشت پائیز میآید. گرما رفته رفته کم میشود، روزها کم کم کوتاه وشبها بلند میگردد[4]. بادهای سرد میوزد، برگها زرد میشود ومیریزد، باد برگهای خشک را بهر طرف میبرد. صفای باغ و بوستان میرود، گرمی و روشنائی خورشید بما کمتر میرسد. با این همه پائیز فصل خوبی است، نه گرم است ونه سرد. میوه های بسیار دارد مانند انگور وسیب وگلابی وبه وانار وخربزه. در پائیز آذوقهٔ زمستان را فراهم میکنند. مردم شهری آرد و برنج وروغن وزغال وهیزم میخرند وانبار میکنند. مردم ده آذوقهٔ خود را از صحرا بخانه میبرند ودر زمینی که شخم کرده اند جو وگندم میکارند. باران میبارد، کشته ها سبز میشود، کم کم هوا روبسردی میرود وزمستان میرسد.

زراعت

زراعت بهترین[5] کارها است. مرد زارع در بهار با گاوآهن زمین شخم میکند. این کار سه فائده دارد. اول، زمین نرم میشود، دوم، زمین زیر

[1]) § 63 (a). — [2]) § 41. 3, *Note 1.* — [3]) § 97 (d). — [4]) § 63 (a). — [5]) § 74 (b).

ورو شده آفتاب میخورد وقوت پیدا میکند، سوم، ریشهٔ علفهای هرزه از زیر خاک بیرون افتاده میخشکد. در پائیز تخم بر زمین می افشانند ودوباره شخم میکنند وماله میکشند تا هموار شود. مرز می بندند که در وقت آبیاری همه جای آن آب میخورد. آرزوی زارع این است که پس از کاشتن تخم وسبز شدن آن باران بیاید. اول تابستان هنگام جو درو است. چند روز بعد گندم میرسد. آن را هم درو میکنند. وقتی که درو تمام شد[1] از جو وگندم خرمن میسازند، خرمن را میکوبند، باد میدهند. باندازهٔ بذر وخوراک یکساله انبار میکنند، باقیمانده را میفروشند واز پول آن چیزهای دیگر میخرند.

لاک پشت وخرگوش

لاک پشتی وخرگوشی در صحرا بهم رسیدند، رفیق[2] راه شدند. خرگوش از راه رفتن لاک پشت بتنگ آمد. گفت این آهسته رفتن تو مارا بمنزل نمیرساند. لاک پشت چون میدانست رفیقش حیوان تنبلی است[3] گفت بیا شرط ببندیم تا کدام یک از ما بآن درختی که بالای تپه است زودتر میرسیم[4]. خرگوش قبول کرد وگفت تو برو ومن هم آمدم[5]. لاک پشت براه افتاد. خرگوش باطمینان تیزپائی خود مشغول چریدن شد. یک مرتبه سرش[6] را بلند کرد. دید نزدیک است[7] لاک پشت برسد. آن وقت پا بدویدن گذاشت ولی هرچه کوشش کرد سودی نبخشید. لاک پشت بدرخت رسیده بود وخرگوش هنوز میدوید.

پوست خرس

دو رفیق با هم قرار گذاشتند بشکار خرس بروند. روزی بطرف جنگل رهسپار شدند وبا هم میگفتند پوست خرس را میفروشیم واز قیمت آن چیزهای خوب میخریم وچنین وچنان میکنیم. اتفاقاً بخرس بزرگ خوش پشمی که از دور میآمد برخوردند. یکی از ترس بالای درختی رفت ودیگری چون تنها ماند وشنیده بود که خرس بمرده کاری ندارد خود را بمردن زد.

[1]) § 81 (b). — [2]) § 68 (b). — [3]) § 97 (a). — [4]) § 63 (c). — [5]) § 81 (d). — [6]) § 77, *Note*. — [7]) § 97 (a).

خرس آمد، اورا بو کرد ورفت. همینکه دور شد آن که بالای درخت بود پائین آمده از رفیقش[1] پرسید که خرس بگوش تو چه گفت؟ جواب داد دو نصیحت کرد یکی آنکه با رفیق ترسو بشکار خرس مرو[2] ودیگر آنکه پوست خرس شکار نکرده مفروش[2].

II

اصلاح وتوسعهٔ کانـــال سوئز

رادیو لندن — خبر نگار[3] روزنامهٔ تایمز لندن از پرت سعید اطلاع میدهد که کمپانی کانال سوئز تصمیم گرفته است اصلاحات مهمی در این کانال بعمل آورد، از جمله بموجب نقشه ای که تنظیم شده است از پرت سعید یک کانال بطول ده کیلومتر حفر کرده[4] وبکانال اصلی ملحق خواهد ساخت واین عمل که دو یا سه سال طول خواهد کشید برای عبور ومرور از کانال تسهیلاتی فراهم خواهد کرد. از طرف دیگر تصمیم گرفته شده است که بر عرض کانال فعلی در تمام طول آن پنجاه سانتیمتر افزوده شود تا کشتی های بزرگ بتوانند[5] براحتی از آن عبور کنند[5] واین کار هم چهار یا پنج سال طول دارد.

بالاخره بمنظور تعمیر راه آهن که از مصر بفلسطین میرود واز روی کانال میگذرد اطلاع داده شده است که در روزهای ۱۸ و۱۹ دسامبر در مدت سی ساعت عبور کشتی ها از کانال متوقف خواهد شد.

دارائی امپراطور ژاپن

توکیو — (خبرگزاری فرانسه.) بالاخره راجع بثروت افسانه آمیز[6] امپراطور ژاپن اطلاعاتی[7] بدست میرسد. بموجب اطلاعاتی که از طرف حکومت ژاپن به ژنرال ماک ارتور داده شده است ثروت میکادو از لحاظ اموال منقول صرف نظر از اشیاء صنعتی وسکه های طلا ونقره وجواهرات ومکنت چهارده تن از شاهزادگان خانوادگی امپراطوری بمبلغی بیش از یک میلیارد

[1]) § 77, *Note.* — [2]) § 40, *Note 1.* — [3]) § 58 (b). — [4]) § 93. I (b). — [5]) § 63 (a), *Note.* — [6]) § 58 (b). — [7]) § 9, *Note.*

ونیم ین بالغ میشود. اموال غیر منقول عبارت اند[1] از سه ملیون اکر زمین که ارزش آنها بیش از سیصد میلیون ین است وجنگل هائی که ششصد ملیون ارزش دارد وعماراتی که ارزش آنها قریب سیصد ملیون می باشد. پول نقد بیش از سیصد ملیون ین است. گذشته از این امپراطور ژاپن بسته های ضخیمی از اسهام بیست ونه شرکت را در دست دارد. ثروت این مرد که متمول ترین[2] شخص دنیا است چه خواهد شد؟ اگر این نکته را در نظر بگیریم که ژاپن فقیر شده[3] وبرای او موضوع غرامات پیش خواهد آمد سؤال فوق شایان توجه میباشد.

تسلط بمب اتمی بر سیـــاست

منچستر — چنانکه خبرگزاری انگلیس گزارش میدهد برتراند روسل فیلسوف معروف انگلیس دیروز در روزنامهٔ منچستر گاردیان راجع به بمب اتمی مقاله ای انتشار داده نوشته است کلیه اختلافات قدیمی بین هندیها ومسلمانان یا بین یهودیان واعراب یا بین انگلیسها وفرانسویان یا بین سوسیالیستها وسرمایه داران در نتیجهٔ تهدید بمب اتمی که بر کلیه محرکین[4] این اختلافات مسلط میباشد وآنهارا به نابودی تهدید مینماید حقیر وناچیز محسوب میشود. امنیت جهان مستلزم انحصار نیروهای مسلح میباشد واین انحصار باید بوسیلهٔ قرارداد عملی گردد ولی عجالةً[5] این سازش غیر ممکن است زیرا دو دولت معظم امریکا واتحاد جماهیر شوروی نمیخواهند در مقابل یکدیگر سر تعظیم فرود آورند. ظاهراً این مسئله از راه عقل وتدبیر حل نخواهد گردید بلکه فقط باید از طرفین[6] زور یا تهدید زور صورت بگیرد. اکنون توفق با امریکا میباشد. بنا بر این ما باید حتی المقدور سعی کنیم که این توفق زیادتر شود تا بحدی که مسئلهٔ انحصار نیروهای مسلح بدون توسل به یک جنگ جدید بین المللی بصورت عمل در آید. اگر این انحصار تحت توجه یک دولت آزادیخواه[7] مانند امریکا تأمین وتضمین گردد این مالیخولیا خاتمه خواهد یافت ومردم جهان دوباره نفس خواهند کشید.

[1]) § 63 (a), *Note*. — [2]) § 74 (a). — [3]) § 93. I (b). — [4]) § 13. A. (a). — [5]) § 6 (d). — [6]) § 13. A. (a), *Note 2*. — [7]) § 58 (b).

نطق چرچیل

لندن — خبرگزاری پارس — مستر چرچیل در ضمن نطقی که در مجلس شورای ملی انگلیس ایراد کرد اظهار نمود روشی را[1] که دولت شوروی در بارهٔ انگلستان پیش گرفته است باعث تأسف همگی اهالی این کشور شده است. سپس اظهار نمود در بین آلمانیها آنهائی که تبه کاران اند باید کیفر شوند ولی نباید از همه ملت انتقام گرفت[2]. مستر چرچیل همچنین اظهارات[3] مستر بوین را در انجمن وزیران خارجه تأیید کرد وگفت مستر بوین صراحةً[4] صحبت کرد ونباید هیچ ملامتی متوجه او گردد. سپس بانتخابات[5] در یونان اشاره نموده گفت پادشاه یونان باید با همه افراد ملت به یکسان رفتار کند وخودش را از روشهای حزبی دور بگیرد. راجع باسپانیا گفت بهتر است مردم آن کشور خودشان راه نجات وخلاصی خود را پیش گیرند. رفتن سفیر کبیر انگلیس از اسپانیا البته چندان تأثیر خوبی در اهالی آنجا نبخشید. راجع بشوروی مستر چرچیل گفت انگلیس از دولت شوروی هیچ نمیخواهد مگر حسن نیت.

بعد از مستر چرچیل مستر اتلی نخست وزیر انگلیس صحبت کرد وراجع به جنوب تیرول گفت ممکن است با مراجعه بآراء عمومی وبسر پرسی دولتهای بزرگ آن نوع حکومتی را که میخواهند بدست بیاورند واز رویه مستر بوین در مذاکرات راجع ببندر تریست تمجید کرد.

مستر مکنیل معاون وزارت خارجه انگلیس از طرف دولت مذاکرات پارلمانی دیروز را بپایان رسانیده وگفت انگلیس در هر مطالبهٔ مشروعی با دولت شوروی موافقت می نماید ولی نمیتوان اصول وهدف های اعلامیه ملل متفق فدا کرد[6]. در موقع کنفرانس پتسدام روسها روحیهٔ مارا درست متوجه نشدند. آلمان باید بتدریج خودشرا خلاص کند ووحدت خودرا ایجاد ودر امور بین المللی بدولتهای بزرگ کمک کند.

فلسطین

اورشلیم — بقرار اظهار خبرگزاری انگلیس نیروی شهربانی نظامی فلسطین در کوههای کارمل واقع در پیرامون حیفا مشغول جستجو میباشند ودر اثنای

[1]) § 98, *Note 1*. — [2]) § 89 (b). — [3]) § 13. A, (b) (ii). — [4]) § 6 (d). — [5]) § 13. A (b) (ii). — [6]) § 89 (b).

کارش دویست نفر یهودی یافتند که بر خلاف مقررات مهاجرت نموده ونیمه شب از بازداشتگاه گریخته اند[1]. مهاجرین بدستیاری اشخاص که از خارج با حیله داخل زندان شده ونگهبان را سرگرم کرده اند[2] موفق بفرار شدند. اینان مهاجرین[3] مزبور را در کامیون گذاشته[4] وبسوی کوهستان بردند. یک دختر جوان یهودی از عزیمت خودداری نمود. لذا اورا سرگرم ساخته وپارچه ای در دهانش فرو بردند تا نتواند نگهبانان را از این واقعه آگاه سازد ولی دختر مزبور بر اثر خفقان در گذشت. در طول راه کارمل کامیونها باتومبیل یک نفر پاسبان بر خوردند واورا هم بهلاکت رسانیدند.

صدها نفر دانشجوی یهودی حیفا امروز بامداد با اتوبوس وکامیون از شهر خارج شدند. احتمال میرود که خروج آنها برای آنست که در صحرا پراکنده گردند واسباب اختلال وبی نظمی فراهم سازند. یک دهکده مجاور که تصور میرفت یهودیان بانجا پناهنده شده اند[5] محاصره شد ولی نظر باینکه اهالی آن دهکده اجتماع کرده[6] وبیم بروز وقایع ناگوار میرفت لذا از محاصرهٔ آن صرف‌نظر گردید.

اورشلیم — بقرار اظهار خبرگزاری فرانسه خبر نگار خبرگزاری مزبور خبر میدهد که وخامت اوضاع حیفا رو بافزایش میرود، بهر دو طرف یعنی دولت ویهودیان نیروی کمکی میرسد. مهاجرین فراری چنین حکایت میکنند که یهودیان در قلهٔ کوه کارمل در جنوب حیفا موضع گرفته اند. هنگامیکه خبر رسید گویا یهودیان مجروح شده باشند[7] صدها[8] نفر از کارگران کارخانجات[9] حیفا بکارمل عزیمت نمودند تا مهاجرین را تقویت کنند. کارخانجات حیفا کار نمیکنند. دستجات[9] دیگر ارتش در پیرامون قلهٔ کارمل گرد آمده هوا پیماهای انگلیس پرواز میکند ومراقب حرکت افراد غیر نظامی میباشند.

دویست نفر از اهالی در اثر هجوم سیل مفقود الاثر[10] گردیده اند

اصفهان — روز ۲۱ آذر سیل مهیبی از کوههای دهستان دهق بطرف دهستان برخوار حمله نموده وشب ۲۲ آذر ابتداء بقراء امیرآباد وحاجی آباد برخورده

1) § 83 (c). — 2) § 83 (c). — 3) § 13. A. (a). — 4) § 93 I (b). — 5) § 97 (a). — 6) § 93 (b). — 7) § 85 (c), *Note 1.* — 8) § 25, *Note 1.* — 9) § 13. A. (b), *Note.* — 10) § 6 (e). —

وخانه های رعایای این هر دو قریه را ویران نموده است، سپس سیل بطرف قصبهٔ گز سرازیر شده وچهار قنات مهم را بکلی خراب نموده ولی دفاع دلیرانهٔ چندین هزار از اهالی خانه های قصبه را از دست برد سیل محفوظ نموده وسیل بطرف قنوات ودهات پائین دست هجوم آورده است. قریه کیونک کاملا ویران شده است، دویست نفر زن وبچه یا بر اثر زیر آوار ماندن ویا بر اثر آب بردن مفقود الاثر گردیده اند وتا پریروز فقط بیست جنازه از زیر آوار خارج شده وفعلاً مشغول تجسس بقیه هستند. بقیه اهالی بالغ بر یک هزار نفر بدون پوشاک وخوراک وساقط از هستی در بیابان سرگردان می باشند. قنات این قریه بکلی منهدم شده است. سیل بعد از اینجا بقریهٔ دست گرد روان شده و۸٦ خانه از این آبادی را ویران نموده واشیاء و آذوقهٔ اهالی را زیر آوار نموده است. قنات این قریه هم بکلی خراب شده است. سیل بعد از این خرابی ها باراضی زیر دست روی آورده وقنات این قریه را هم خراب میماید ولی در این محل تلفات جانی وارد نشده است. از اطراف زیر دست در حدود بیست قنات از قریهٔ دولت آباد ومزارع آن وچند قنات دیگر از قریهٔ خورزوق کاملا ویران شده است. آنچه که[1] تا کنون تخمین زده شده صدی نود از قنوات این نواحی حاصل خیز بکلی ویران شده وبالغ بر ۱۵۰ میلیون ریال خسارت وارد شده است. رویهم رفته در حدود بیست هزار نفر در اثر این سیل یا بی خانمان شده و یا آسیب دیده اند. وسیلهٔ امرار معاش چند هزار زارع بدبخت از بین رفته است.

در هندوستان یک پالایشگاه تأسیس میشود

دهلی جدید ــ دولت هندوستان قراردادی با کمپانی نفت استاندارد واکیوم امریکا امضاء کرده[2] که بموجب آن کمپانی مزبور در ظرف تقریباً چهار سال یک پالایشگاه بمبلغ ۳۵ میلیون دلار در بمبئی تأسیس کند. قرارداد مزبور ضمن مبادلهٔ نامه هائی که متضمن مواد قرار داد است منعقد شده است. بموجب این قرارداد پالایشگاه مزبور یک میلیون تن نفت تصفیه خواهد نمود ومحصولات آن عبارت خواهد بود از بنزین کروسین وروغن دیزل. دولت هندوستان موافقت کرده[3] امتیازاتی از لحاظ حقوق وعوارض گمرکی به

[1]) § 98, *Note 2.* — [2]) § 37. 1, *Note.* — [3]) § 37. 1, *Note.*

کمپانی مزبور بدهد ومدت ۲۵ سال از ملی کردن تصفیه خانه خودداری نماید. استاندارد واکیوم موظف است طبق قرارداد منعقده افراد هندی را برای اداره تصفیه خانه تربیت کند ودر صورتیکه حد کافی متخصصین[1] هندی تربیت شوند از وجود آنها در ادارهٔ امور پالایشگاه استفاده نماید. شرکت استاندارد واکیوم مبلغ ۲٫۵۰۰٫۰۰۰ روپیه برای ساختمان خانه های مسکونی برای کارگران هندی تخصیص خواهد داد. اگر پس از بیست وپنج سال دولت هندوستان بخواهد صنعت نفت خود را ملی نماید باندازهٔ کافی جبران خسارات وارده[2] را خواهد کرد. شرکت استاندارد واکیوم از بعضی قوانین ومقررات مربوط بصنایع هندوستان مستثنی خواهد بود. وسایل کافی برای وارد کردن ماشین ها وکار خانهٔ مورد نیاز با ۵۰٫۲۵ در صد عوارض گمرکی از هم اکنون آماده شده است. تا مدتی که هنوز نفت خام در هندوستان استخراج نشده است شرکت استاندارد واکیوم اجازه خواهد داشت نفت خام مورد نیاز را بدون پرداخت عوارض گمرکی از خارج وارد کند. دولت هندوستان ضمناً موافقت کرده است که بنادر ووسایل بارگیری واسکلهٔ کافی ووسایل حمل ونقل زمینی تهیه نماید.

III

غوزه

گنجشکی بود، بالای دیوار بلندی لانه داشت. روزی توی بیابان دنبال آب ودانه میگشت که[3] باد از پنبه زار یک پنبه دانه آورد وجلوش بر زمین زد. گنجشک زود آنرا بنوکش گرفت وبرد توی لانه اش[4]. بهمسایه اش[5] نشان داد وگفت این چیه[6]؟ گفت این پنبه دانه است. پرسید بچه درد میخورد؟ جواب داد این را می کارند، غوزه در میآید، غوزه را می شکنند، پنبه میشود، پنبه را می ریسند، نخ میشود، نخ را می بافند پارچه میشود، پارچه رنگ می کنند، رنگی میشود، می دوزند قبا میشود، بر تن ما وشما میشود. گنجشگ خوشحال شد وپنبه دانه را بر داشت، آمد توی

[1]) § 13. A (a). — [2]) § 71. — [3]) § 97 (d), *Note*. — [4]) § 61, *Note 3*. — [5]) § 77, Note. — [6]) *čīye* = *čīst*, from *čī* = *če* (§ 22 (2)) and *-e* = *ast* (§ 41. 1, *Note*).

کشت[1]، دید کشاورزی دارد[2] زمین را بیل میزند، که تخم بکارد. گفت کارکار، این را بکار، نیم از تو، نیم از من. کشاورز گفت خیلی خوب. کاشت وبعد از مدتی سبز شد ورسید. غوزه هارا کند ودو رسد کرد، یکیش[3] را برای خودش نگاهداشت ویکی را هم بگنجشک داد. گنجشک خوشحال شد، آنها را بر داشت وآورد دکان[4] نخ تاب[5]. گفت ریس ریس، اینها را بریس، نیم از تو، نیم از من. نخ تاب گفت خیلی خوب. گرفت، ریسید، دور چوبی پیچید. رسد خودشرا بر داشت ورسد گنجشکه[6] را هم داد. گنجشک خوشحال شد. نخ ها را آورد در دکان شعر باف[7]. گفت باف باف، اینهارا بباف، نیم از تو، نیم از من. شعر باف گفت خیلی خوب. بافت ومال خودش را بر داشت ومال گنجشک را هم داد. گنجشک خوشحال شد وپارچه را بر داشت، آورد در دکان رنگ رزی[7]، گفت رنگ رنگ، اینهارا برنگ، نیم از تو، نیم از من. گفت خیلی خوب. رنگ رز اینهارا رنگ آبی آسمانی کرد وانداخت روی بند توی آفتاب[7] که[8] خشک بشود. گنجشکه[9] آمد، دید وبا خودش گفت به به، چه رنگ قشنگی است. حیف است که پارچهٔ باین خوش رنگی را بدهم برنگ رز[10]، بهتر است تا سر رنک رز گرم است[11] پارچه هارا از روی بند ور دارم، در برم. یواشکی آمد، پارچه هارا بنوک گرفت وپرید، رفت. نا پرید[12] رنک رز فهمید، دوید آمد، گفت ای گنجشک مگر نگفتی نیم از تو، نیم از من؟ پس رسد من کو؟ گفت کی[13] گفت؟ کی کرد؟ گنجشک پارچه هارا بر داشت وآورد پهلوی درزی[14]. گفت دوز دوز، اینها را بدوز، یکی از تو، یکی از من. درزی هم دو تا جبهٔ قشنگ دوخت، بچوب آویزان کرد. گنجشک از دور دید، با خودش گفت حیف نیست جبهٔ باین خوبی را بدهم بدزری[15]؟ هر دوش[16] برای خودم خوبست. وقتی که درزی با چوب داشت[17] اندازهٔ یکی را میگرفت گنجشک یواشکی پرید ودو تا جبه را بنوک گرفت ورفت. درزی هرچه صدا زد وگفت مگر نگفتی یکی از تو، یکی از من؟ گنجشک گفت ای بابا، کی گفت

[1]) § 61. *Note 3.* — [2]) § 80 (a), *Note.* — [3]) § 17, *Note 2.* — [4]) § 45, *Note 1.* — [5]) § 61, *Note 3.* — [6]) § 8, *Note.* — [7]) § 61, *Note 3.* — [8]) § 97 (b). — [9]) § 8, *Note.* — [10]) § 61, *Note 3.* — [11]) § 96 (c). — [12]) § 96 (d). — [13]) § 22 (1). — [14]) § 61, *Note 3.* — [15]) § 61, *Note 3.* — [16]) § 17, *Notes 1* and *2.* — [17]) § 82 (a), *Note.*

کی[1] کرد ؟ گنجشک جبه هارا آورد پهلوی ملا[2]. گفت ای ملا، میخواهم دو تا جبه پهلوت امانت بگذارم تا وقتی هوا سرد میشود ازت[3] بگیرم. مزد امانت داری هم این که یکیش[4] از تو باشد ویکیش[4] از من. ملا گفت خیلی خوب، اینها را نگه میدارم، هوا که[5] سرد شد یکیشرا خودم می پوشم، یکیشرا هم میدهم بتو[6]. ملا جبه هارا نگاهی کرد وبا خودش گفت حیف نیست که یکیش را بدهم باین گنجشک جیر جیری، هر دوش[7] را برای خودم نگه میدارم. روزها گذشت. باد خشک وزید. هوا رو بسردی رفت. گنجشک یاد جبه ها افتاد. پا شد، آمد خانهٔ ملا[8]. ملا تا دید[9] گنجشک میآید[10] بسراغش[11] رفت سر نماز[11]. گنجشک آنقدر ایستاد تا نمازش تمام شد[12]. گفت ملا، جبهٔ مرا بده. گفت کدام جبه ؟ گفت همان دو تا جبه ای که پهلوت[13] امانت گذاشتم، خودت هم گفتی یکی مال تو، یکیش هم مال من. گفت کی[14] گفت ؟ کی[14] کرد ؟ گنجشک گفت هوا سرد میشود من هم سرما میخورم. گفت من دعا میخوانم سرما نخوری. گفت من دعا نمیخواهم، قبا میخواهم. ملا دوباره رفت سر نماز[15]. گنجشک هم نا امید شد و رفت. اما دور وبر خانهٔ ملا می پلکید تا یک روزی که[16] از دور دید ملا جبه هارا آب کشیده[17] که پاک بشود[18] وبتواند بپوشد[18] و روی بند انداخته که خشک بشود وخودش هم رفته سر نماز[19]. یک هو پرید واز روی بند جبه هارا ور داشت ورفت. تا ملا دید[20] نماز را شکست وفریاد زد آهای گنجشکه[21]، جبه هارا کجا میبری؟ حرف خودت را قبول دارم، یکیش ازمن یکیش ازتو. گنجشک گفت کی گفت؟ کی کرد؟ دو روز بعدش دوباره آمد بسراغ خانهٔ ملا[22]. دید ملا عمامه اش را ور داشته لب حوض گذاشته ودارد[23] دست نماز میگیرد. پرید، عمامهٔ ملا را ور داشت. ملا صدا داد بابا، عمامه را کجا می بری؟ توی سرما سرم یخ میکند. گفت دعا میکنم سرت یخ نکند. باری گنجشک عمامهٔ ملا را آورد، لانهٔ بچه هاش[24] کرد. بعد باین فکر افتاد که جبه ها را ببازار ببرد

[1]) § 22 (1). — [2]) § 61, *Note 3.* — [3]) § 76, *Note 1.* — [4]) § 17, *Note 2.* — [5]) § 97 (d). — [6]) § 61, *Note 3.* — [7]) (§ 17, *Notes 1* and *2.* — [8]) § 61, *Note 3.* — [9]) § 96 (d). — [10]) § 97 (a) — [11]) § 61. *Note 3.* — [12]) § 96 (a). — [13]) § 17, *Note 1.* [14]) § 22 (1). — [15]) § 61, *Note 3.* — [16]) § 97 (d), *Note.* — [17]) § 37.1, *Note.* — [18]) § 97 (b). — [19]) § 61, *Note 3.* — [20]) § 96 (d). — [21]) § 8, *Note.* — [22]) § 61. *Note 3.* — [23]) § 80 (a), *Note.* — [24]) § 17, *Note 1.*

وبفروشد ودان برای زمستان بگیرد. میان راه باد وبوران سختی در گرفت. باد افتاد زیر این دو تا جبه(1 واز نوک گنجشک در آمد. گنجشک هر کاری کرد خودش را برساند وجبه هارا بگیرد نتوانست. باد یکی از این دو جبه را آورد، انداخت جلو دکان درزی(1. همان درزی که جبه هارا دوخته بود. ویکی را هم جلو دکان رنک رز(2. همان رنگ رزی که پارچه اش را رنگ کرده بود. بالا رفتیم آرد بود، پائین آمدیم خمیر بود، قصهٔ ما همین بود.

پیره زن

یکی بود یکی نبود(3، یک پیره زن بود. خانه ای داشت باندازهٔ یک غربیل. اطاقی داشت باندازهٔ یک بشقاب. درخت سنجدی داشت باندازهٔ یک چیلهٔ جارو. یک خرده هم جل وجهاز سر هم کرده بود که رف وطاقچه اش خشک وخالی نباشد(4.

یک شب شامش(5 را خورده بود که(6 دید باد سردی میآید وتنش مورمور میشود(7. رختخابش(8 را انداخت ورفت توش(9 هنوز چشم بهم نگذاشته بود که(10 دید صدای در میآید(11. شمع را ور داشت ورفت در را وا کرد. دید یک گنجشکی است(11. گنجشک به پیره زن گفت پیره زن، امشب هوا سرد است، باد میآید، من هم جائی ندارم. بگذار امشب اینجا پهلوی تو توی این خانه بمانم، صبح که(12 آفتاب زد میپرم، میروم. پیره زن دلش بحال گنجشکه سوخت(13 وگفت خیلی خوب، بیا تو(14، برو روی درخت سنجد لای برگها(15 بگیر بخواب. گنجشکه(16 را خواباند وخودش رفت توی رختخواب. هنوز چشمش گرم نشده بود که(17 دید باز در میزنند(18. رفت دم در(19 ، در را وا کرد ، دید یک خری است(20. خره(21 گفت امشب هوا سرد است، باد هم میآید، من هم جائی ندارم که سرم را بگذارم راحت بخوابم، بگذار امشب اینجا توی خانهٔ تو بمانم، صبح زود پیش از آنکه صدای

1) § 61, *Note 3.* — 2) § 61, *Note 3.* — 3) The traditional formula at the beginning of folktales corresponding to the English "Once upon a time...", *lit.* "There was someone (God), there was no one (else)." — 4) § 97 (b). — 5) § 77, *Note.* — 6) § 97 (d), *Note.* — 7) § 97 (a). — 8) § 77, *Note.* — 9) § 17, *Note 1.* — 10) § 97 (d), *Note.* — 11) § 97 (a). — 12) § 97 (d). — 13) § 61, *Note 2.* — 14) § 61, *Note 3.* — 15) § 61, *Note 3.* — 16) § 8, *Note.* — 17) § 97 (d), *Note.* — 18) § 97 (a). — 19) § 61, *Note 3.* — 20) § 97 (a). — 21) § 8, *Note.*

اذان از گلدسته بلند بشود[1] من میروم بیرون[2]. پیره زن دلش بحال خره[3] سوخت[4] وگفت خیلی خوب، برو گوشهٔ حیاط[5]، بگیر بخواب. پیره زن خررا خواباند ورفت خودش هم خوابید. بازم[6] دید در میزنند، گفت کیه[7]؟ ورفت دم در[8]، دید یک مرغی است[9]. مرغه[10] گفت پیره زن، امشب باد میآید وهوا سرد است، من هم راه بردار بجائی نیستم، بگذار بیایم امشب اینجا بخوابم. صبح زود همین که صدای خروس در آمد[11] من پا میشوم میروم. پیره زن گفت خیلی خوب، برو کنج حیاط[12] بگیر بخواب. مرغ را خواباند وخودش رفت که[13] بخوابد، دید صدای در میآید[14]. آمد در را وا کرد. دید یک کلاغی است[14]. کلاغه[15] گفت پیره زن، امشب هوا سرد است، من هم جای درست وحسابی ندارم، بگذار اینجا توی خانهٔ تو بخوابم. صبح زود همین که مرغها سر از لانه در آوردند[16]، میپرم میروم. گفت خیلی خوب وکلاغه[17] را برد، روی گرده خره خواباند ورفت خوابید. دید باز هم در میزنند[18]. شمع را ور داشت، رفت دم در، دید سگی است[18]. گفت چه میگوئی ؟ گفت امشب هوا سرد است، من هم خانه ولانه ای ندارم که پناه برم توش[19]. بگذار امشب اینجا بخوابم. صبح پیش از آنکه بوق حمام را بزنند[20] پا میشوم میروم. پیره زن دلش برای سگه سوخت[21]، آنرا برد پهلوی خر خواباند و، گوش شیطان کر، آمد خوابید. صبح که[22] از خواب بیدار شد دید خانه اش غلغلهٔ روم است[23]. رفت بسراغ گنجشکه[24]، گفت پا شو، برو بیرون که[25] صبح شد. کنجشکه گفت من، که جیک جیک میکنم برات[26]، تخم کوچیک میکنم برات[26]، من برم[27] بیرون ؟ پیره زن گفت نه، تو بمان. رفت بسراغ خره[28]، گفت زود باش، پا شو، برو بیرون، صبح شده[29]. خره گفت من، که عرعر میکنم برات[30]، پشکل تر میکنم برات[31]، همسایه خبر میکنم برات[31]. من برم[32] بیرون ؟ پیره زن گفت

1) § 85 (g). — 2) § 61, *Note 3.* — 3) § 8, *Note.* — 4) § 61, *Note* 2. — 5) § 61, *Note* 3. — 6) *bāzam* = *bāz ham* (§ 2, *Note* on ه *h*). — 7) *kīye* = *kīst*, from *kī* = *ke* (§ 22 (1) and *-e* = *ast* (§ 41. 1. *Note*). — 8) § 61, *Note 3.* — 9) § 97 (a). — 10) § 8, *Note.* — 11) § 81 (b). — 12) § 61, *Note 3.* — 13) § 97 (b), — 14) § 97 (a). — 15) § 8, *Note.* — 16) § 81 (b). — 17) § 8, *Note.* — 18) § 97 (a). — 19) § 17, *Note 1.* — 20) § 85 (g). — 21) § 61, *Note 2.* — 22) § 97 (d). — 23) § 97 (a). — 24) § 8, *Note.* — 25) § 97 (c). — 26) § 17, *Note 1.* — 27) *beram* = *beravam* (§ 5 (d), *Note* (d)). — 28) § 8, *Note.* — 29) § 37. 1, *Note.* — 30) § 17, *Note 1.* — 31) § 17, *Note 1.* — 32) *beram* = *beravam* (§ 5 (d), *Note* (d)).

نه، تو هم بمان. رفت پیش مرغه[1]، گفت یالا، پا شو، برو بیرون، که[2] صبح شده[3]. مرغه گفت من، که قد قد میکنم برات، تخم بزرگ میکنم برات، من برم بیرون؟ گفت نه، تو هم بمان. رفت بسراغ کلاغه[4]. گفت پا شو، بیرون برو. کلاغه گفت من، که قار قار میکنم برات. آقارا بیدار میکنم برات، من برم بیرون؟ گفت نه، تو هم بمان. آخر سر آمد بسراغ سگه[4]، گفت پا شو، برو بیرون، که[5] هوا روشن شده[6]. سگه گفت من، که واق واق میکنم برات، دزد را بیدماغ میکنم برات، من برم بیرون؟ گفت نه، تو هم بمان. همه آنجا ماندند وکارهای پیره زن را رو براه کردند وزندگیش را روی غلتک انداختند. قصهٔ ما بسر رسید، کلاغه بخانه اش نرسید.

[1]) § 8, *Note.* — [2]) § 97 (c). — [3]) § 37. 1, *Note.* — [4]) § 8, *Note.* — [5]) § 97 (c). — [6]) § 27. 1, *Note.*

Vocabulary

آب *āb* water. *āb kašīdan* to rinse.

آبادی *ābādī* village.

آبی *ābī* blue. *ābī-āsemānī* sky-blue.

آبیاری *ābyārī* irrigation.

آخر *āxer* last. *āxer-e sar* in the end.

آذر *āẕar* the ninth month of the Persian year (November-December).

آذوقه *āẕuqe* provisions.

آراء *ārā'* votes. (Pl. of *ra'y*.)

آرد *ārd* flour.

آرزو *ārzū* wish, desire.

آزادیخواه *āzādīxvāh* democratic.

آسوده *āsūde* quiet, at rest.

آسیا *āsiyā* mill.

آسیب *āsīb* damage.

آفتاب *āftāb* sun. *āftāb xordan* to be exposed to the sun.

آقا *āqā* gentleman.

آگاه *āgāh* informed, aware.

آلمان *ālmān* Germany.

آلمانی *ālmānī* German.

آماده *āmāde* prepared.

آمدن *āmadan* to come.

آنجا *ānǰā* there.

آوار *āvār* ruins.

آوردن *āvordan* to bring.

آویزان *āvīzān* hanging, suspended.

آهای *āhāi̯* hey!

آهسته *āheste* slow(ly).

آهو *āhū* gazelle.

ابتداءً *ebtedā'an* in the beginning.

ابریشم *abrīšom* silk.

اتحاد *etteḥād* union.

اتفاقا *ettefāqan* by chance.

اتلی *atlī* Attlee.

اتمی *atomī* atomic.

اتوبوس *otobūs* omnibus.

اتوموبیل *otomobīl* motor car.

اثر *aṡar* trace. *bar aṡar-e* as the result of.

اثنا *aṡnā* interval. *dar aṡnā-ye* during.

اجازه *eǰāze* permission.

اجتماع *eǰtemā'* (act of) meeting, gathering together.

احتمال *eḥtemāl* possibility, *eḥtemāl mīravad* it is possible.

اختلاف *extelāf* difference, dispute.

اختلال *extelāl* confusion.

اداره *edāre* administration.

اذان *aẕān* call to prayer.

اراضی *arāẓī* lands, territories. (Pl. of *arẓ*.)

ارتش *arteš* army.

ارزش *arzeš* value.

ارزن *arzan* millet.

اسب *asb* horse.

اسباب *asbāb* causes. (Pl. of *sabab*.)

اسپانیا *espāniyā* Spain.

استاندارد واکیوم *estāndārd vākyūm* Standard Vacuum.

استخراج *estexrāǰ* extraction, exploitation.

استفاده *estefāde* (act of) taking advantage, utilizing.

اسکله *eskele* pier, jetty, quay.

اسم *esm* name.

اسهام *ashām* shares. (Pl. of *sahm*.)

اشاره *ešāre* reference.

اشخاص *ašxāṣ* persons. (Pl. of *šaxs*.)

اشیاء *ašyā'* things. (Pl. of *šei̯'*.)

اصفهان *eṣfahān* Isfahan.

اصلاح *eṣlāḥ* reform, improvement.

اصلی *aṣlī* original; principal, main.

اصول *oṣūl* principles. (Pl. of *aṣl*.)

اطاق *oṭāq* room.

اطراف *aṭrāf* sides; outskirts. (Pl. of *ṭaraf*.)

اطلاع *eṭṭelāʿ* information. *eṭṭelāʿ dādan* to state.

اطمینان *eṭmīnān* confidence, trust, reliance.

اظهار *eẓhār* statement.

اعراب *aʿrāb* Arabs. (Pl. of *ʿarab*.)

اعلامیه *eʿlāmīye* declaration.

اغلب *aɣlab* the most part, most.

افتادن *oftādan* to fall.

افراد *afrād* individuals. (Pl. of *fard*.)

افزایش *afzāyeš* increase.

افزودن *afzūdan* to increase.

افسانه آمیز *afsāne-āmīz* fabulous.

افشاندن *afšāndan* to scatter.

اکر *akr* acre.

اکنون *aknūn* now.

البته *albatte* of course.

اما *ammā* but.

امانت *amānat* deposit. *amānat gozāštan* to deposit.

امانت داری *amānat-dārī* safe-keeping.

امپراطور *emperāṭūr* emperor.

امپراطوری *emperāṭūrī* imperial.

امتیاز *emtiyāz* concession.

امرار *emrār* (act of) earning (one's livelihood).

امروز *emrūz* to-day.

امریکا *emrīkā* America.

امشب *emšab* to-night.

امضاء *emẓāʾ* signature.

امنیت *amnīyat* security.

اموال *amvāl* goods. (Pl. of *māl*.)

امور *omūr* affairs, matters. (Pl. of *amr*.)

امیر آباد *amīr-ābād* Amirabad.

انار *anār* pomegranate.

انبار *anbār* store, granary.

انتخابات *entexābāt* general election.

انتشار *entešār* (state of) being published. *entešār dādan* to publish.

انتقام *enteqām* revenge, vengeance.

انجمن *anǰoman* assembly, council.

انحصار *enḥeṣār* restriction.

انداختن *andāxtan* to throw, to throw down.

اندازه *andāze* measure, extent, size.

انس *ons* familiarity. *ons gereftan* to become tame.

انسان *ensān* man.

انگلستان *englestān* England, Great Britain.

انگلیس *englīs* England, Great Britain; English, British.

انگور *angūr* grape.

اورشلیم *ūršelīm* Jerusalem.

اوضاع *ouẓāʿ* conditions, state of affairs. (Pl. of *vaẓʿ*.)

اول *avval* first; beginning.

اهالی *ahālī* population. (Pl. of *ahl*.)

اهل *ahl* people.

ایجاد *īǰād* creation, establishment.

ایراد *īrād* delivery (of a speech).

ایران *īrān* Persia.

ایستادن *īstādan* to stand.

اینجا *īnǰā* here.

ب

بابا *bābā* father.

باد *bād* wind. *bād dādan* to winnow.

بار *bār* burden, load.

باران *bārān* rain.

بارکش *bār-kaš* load-carrying. *asb-e bār-kaš* pack-horse.

بارگیری *bārgīrī* (act of) loading.

باره *bāre* respect. *dar bāre-ye* with respect to.
باری *bārī* anyhow.
باریدن *bārīdan* to rain.
باز *bāz* again.
بازار *bāzār* market, bazaar.
بازداشتگاه *bāzdāštgāh* concentration camp.
باعث *bā'es̱* cause.
باغ *bāγ* garden.
بافتن *bāftan* to weave.
باقیمانده *bāqīmānde* remainder.
بال *bāl* wing.
بالا *bālā* above, up. *bālā-ye* up.
بالاخره *be'l-axere* at last.
بالغ *bāleγ* amounting. *bāleγ šodan* to amount.
بامداد *bāmdād* in the morning.
بچه *bačče* child, young (one).
بخشیدن *baxšīdan* to present; to produce.
بدبخت *badbaxt* unfortunate.
بدون *bedūn-e* without.
بذر *baẕr* seed.
برابر *barābar* equal, opposite. *dar barābar-e* opposite, against.
برای *barā-ye* for. *az barā-ye* id.
برتراند روسل *berterānd rūsel* Bertrand Russell.
برخوار *borxvār* Borkhar.
بر خوردن *bar-xordan* to meet, come in contact with.
بر داشتن *bar-dāštan* to pick up.
بردن *bordan* to take, carry (away).
برزگر *barzgar* cultivator.
برگ *barg* leaf.
برنج *berenǰ* rice.
بروز *borūz* appearance, outbreak.
بره *barre* lamb.
بزرگ *bozorg* great, large, big.
بستن *bastan* to bind, tie; to close.
بسته *baste* package, bundle.
بشر *bašar* mankind.
بشقاب *bošqāb* plate.
بع بع *ba'-ba'* (sound of) bleating.
بعد *ba'd* afterwards.
بعضی *ba'ẓī* some.
بقیه *baqīye* rest, remainder.
بلکه *balke* but.
بلند *boland* high, tall; long. *boland kardan* to raise. *boland šodan* to rise.
بمب *bomb* bomb.
بمبئی *bamba'ī* Bombay.
بنا *benā* building. *benā bar in* therefore.
بنادر *banāder* ports, harbours. (Pl. of *bandar*).
بند *band* clothes-line.
بندر *bandar* port, harbour.
بنزین *benzin* petrol.
بو *bū* smell. *bū kardan* to smell.
بوران *būrān* squall.
بوستان *būstān* garden.
بوق *būq* horn, bugle.
بوین *bevin* Bevin.
به *beh* quince.
بهار *bahār* spring.
به به *bah-bah* bravo!
بیابان *biyābān* desert.
بی خانمان *bī-xānemān* homeless.
بیدار *bīdār* awake. *bīdār šodan* to wake up.
بیدماغ *bīdamāγ* annoyed.
بیرون *bīrūn* out.
بیست *bīst* twenty.
بیل *bīl* spade. *bīl zadan* to break up (with a spade).
بیم *bīm* fear.
بین *bein* interval. *dar bein-e* amongst. *az bein raftan* to be lost.
بین المللی *beino'l-melalī* international.
بی نظمی *bī-naẓmī* disorder.
بینی *bīnī* nose.

پ

پا *pā* foot; hind leg. *pā šodan* to rise, get up.
پادشاه *pādšāh* king.
پارچه *pārče* cloth.
پارلمانی *pārlemānī* parliamentary.
پارس *pārs* Pars.
پاسبان *pāsbān* policeman.
پاک *pāk* pure, clean.
پالایشگاه *pālāyešgāh* refinery.
پالوده *pālūde* name of a sweet beverage.
پایان *pāyān* end, conclusion.
پائیز *pā'īz* autumn.
پائین *pā'in* below, down.
پائین دست *pā'in-dast* lower.
پتسدام *potsdām* Potsdam.
پختن *poxtan* to cook, bake.
پر *par* feather; wing.
پراکنده *parākande* scattered.
پرت سعید *port sa'īd* Port Said.
پرداخت *pardāxt* payment.
پر زور *por-zūr* powerful, strong
پرسیدن *porsīdan* to ask.
پرنده *parande* flying creature; bird.
پرواز *parvāz* flight.
پروانه *parvāne* butterfly, moth.
پریدن *parīdan* to fly.
پریروز *parīrūz* the day before yesterday.
پشت *pošt* back.
پشکل *peškel* orbicular dung.
پشم *pašm* wool.
پشمی *pašmī* woollen.
پل *pol* bridge.
پلکیدن *palakīdan* to loaf about.
پناه *panāh* refuge. *panāh bordan* to take refuge.
پناهنده *panāhande* refugee.
پنبه *panbe* cotton.
پنبه دانه *panbe-dāne* cotton-seed.
پنبه زار *panbe-zār* cotton-field.
پنج *panǰ* five.
پنجاه *panǰāh* fifty.
پنیر *panīr* cheese.
پوست *pūst* skin, hide.
پوشاک *pūšāk* clothing.
پوشیدن *pūšīdan* to wear, put on.
پول *pūl* money.
پهلو *pahlū* side. *pahlū-ye* beside; towards, to.
پیچیدن *pīčīdan* to wind, twist.
پیدا *peidā* visible. *peidā kardan* to find.
پیر *pīr* old.
پیرامون *pīrāmūn* environs.
پیراهن *pīrāhan* shirt.
پیره زن *pīre-zan* old woman.
پیش *pīš* before (adv.). *pīš az ānke* before (conj.).
پیش آمدن *pīš-āmadan* to come up, arise, occur.
پیش گرفتن *pīš-gereftan* to adopt, follow.
پیله *pīle* cocoon.

ت

تابستان *tābestān* summer.
تأثیر *ta'ṯīr* impression.
تار *tār* warp.
تأسف *ta'assof* regret.
تأسیس *ta'sīs* foundation, establishment.
تأمین *ta'mīn* security, guarantee.
تایمز *tāimz* the Times.
تأئید *ta'īd* support, confirmation.
تبه کار *tabah-kār* criminal.
تپه *tappe* hill.
تجسس *taǰassos* investigation.
تخت *taxt* throne.
تخصیص *taxṣīṣ* appropriation, allotment. *taxsīs dādan* to appropriate, allot.
تخم *toxm* seed; egg.
تخمین *taxmin* estimate. *taxmin zadan* to estimate.
تدبیر *tadbīr* prudence.

تدریج *tadrīǰ* gradation. *betadrīǰ* gradually.
تر *tar* moist; fresh.
تربیت *tarbiyat* training, cultivation; production.
ترس *tars* fear.
ترسو *tarsū* cowardly.
ترش *torš* sour; fermented.
تریست *triyest* Trieste.
تسلط *tasallot̤* domination.
تسهیل *tashīl* facility.
تصفیه *taṣfiye* (act of) refining.
تصفیه خانه *taṣfiye-xāne* refinery.
تصمیم *taṣmīm* decision. *taṣmīm gereftan* to decide.
تصور *taṣavvor* imagination, thought.
تضمین *taẓmīn* guarantee.
تعظیم *taʿẓīm* homage.
تعمیر *taʿmīr* (act of) repairing.
تقریباً *taqrīban* approximately.
تقویت *taqviyat* reinforcement.
تلف *talaf* loss.
تمام *tamām* whole, all. *tamām šodan* to be completed finished.
تمجید *tamǰīd* praise.
تن *tan* body; person.
تن *ton* ton.
تنبل *tanbal* lazy.
تنظیم *tanẓīm* arrangement, organization.
تنگ *tang* narrow. *betang āmadan* to be annoyed.
تنور *tanūr* oven.
تنوری *tanūrī* baked in an oven.
تنها *tanhā* alone.
تنیدن *tanīdan* to spin.
تو *tū* inside; in. *tū-ye* in, into.
توانستن *tavānestan* to be able.
توت *tūt* mulberry.
توجه *tavaǰǰoh* attention.
توسعه *touseʿe* expansion, development.
توسل *tavassol* resort, recourse.
توفق *tavaffoq* superiority.
توکیو *tokyo* Tokyo.
تهدید *tahdīd* threat.
تهیه *tahīye* preparation, provision.
تیرول *tīrol* Tyrol.
تیز پائی *tīz-pā'ī* fleet-footedness.

ث

ثروت *s̱arvat* wealth.

ج

جا *ǰā* place.
جارو *ǰārū* (coll. for جاروب *ǰārūb*) broom.
جانی *ǰānī* pertaining to life.
جبران *ǰabrān* compensation.
جبه *ǰobbe* cloak.
جدا *ǰodā* separated. *ǰodā kardan* to separate.
جدید *ǰadīd* new.
جستجو *ǰostoǰu* search.
جل و جهاز *ǰol o ǰahāz* furniture.
جلو *ǰelou̯* bridle. *ǰelou̯-e* in front of.
جماهیر *ǰamāhīr* republics. (Pl. of *ǰomhūr*.)
جمع *ǰamʿ* collection, assembly.
جمله *ǰomle* totality, whole. *az ǰomle* amongst other things.
جنازه *ǰanāze* corpse.
جنگ *ǰang* war, battle. *ǰang kardan* to fight.
جنگل *ǰangal* forest.
جنوب *ǰanūb* south.
جو *ǰou̯* barley.
جواب *ǰavāb* reply, answer. *ǰavāb dādan* to reply.
جوان *ǰavān* young.
جواهرات *ǰavāherāt* jewels.
جو درو *ǰou̯-derou̯* season for reaping barley.
جوراب *ǰūrāb* stocking.
جهاز *ǰahāz* See جل و جهاز *ǰol o ǰahāz*.

جهان *ǰahān* world.
جیر جیری *ǰīr-ǰīrī* chattering.
جیک جیک *ǰīk-ǰīk* (sound of) chirping.

چ

چربی *čarbī* fat, grease.
چرچیل *čorčīl* Churchill.
چریدن *čarīdan* to graze.
چسبیدن *časbīdan* to stick, adhere
چشم *čašm* eye.
چنان *čonān* } such; thus.
چنین *čonin* } such; thus.
چند *čand* several; how much?
چندان *čandān* such.
چندین *čandin* so many; many.
چوب *čūb* stick.
چهار *čahār* four.
چهارده *čahārdah* fourteen.
چیز *čīz* thing.
چیله *čīle* chip.

ح

حاجی آباد *ḥāǰī-ābād* Hajiabad.
حاصل خیز *ḥāṣel-xīz* fertile.
حاضر *ḥāẓer* ready.
حال *ḥāl* condition.
حتّی المقدور *ḥatta'lmaqdūr* as much as possible.
حد *ḥadd* limit, extent.
حدود *ḥodūd* limits. (Pl. of *ḥadd*.) *dar ḥodud-e* about.
حرارت *ḥarārat* heat.
حرف *ḥarf* letter; word.
حرکت *ḥarakat* movement.
حریر *ḥarīr* silk.
حریره *ḥarīre* name of a sweet made out of flour and milk.
حزبی *ḥezbī* pertaining to a party.
حسابی *ḥesābī* proper.
حسن *ḥosn* beauty. *ḥosn-e nīyat* good will.
حفر *ḥafr* digging, excavation.
حقوق *ḥoqūq* rights, dues. (Pl. of *ḥaqq*.)
حقیر *ḥaqīr* mean, contemptible.
حکایت *ḥekāyat* story, tale. *ḥekāyat kardan* to relate.
حکومت *ḥokūmat* government.
حل *ḥall* solution.
حمام *ḥammām* public bath. *būq-e hammām* the horn announcing that the bath is open.
حمل *ḥaml* transport. *haml o naql* id.
حمله *ḥamle* attack.
حوض *ḥouẓ* tank, pool.
حیاط *ḥayāṭ* courtyard.
حیف *ḥeif* pity.
حیفا *ḥeifā* Haifa.
حیله *ḥīle* trick.
حیوان *ḥeivān* animal.
حیوانک *ḥeivānak* little animal.

خ

خاتمه *xāteme* conclusion, end.
خارج *xāreǰ* going out; external, outside, abroad. *xāreǰ šodan* to go out, emerge.
خارجه *xāreǰe* in *omūr-e xāreǰe* foreign affairs. (Fem. of *xāreǰ*.)
خاک *xāk* soil.
خالص *xāleṣ* pure.
خالی *xālī* empty. *xošk o xālī* id.
خام *xām* raw, crude.
خانوادگی *xānevādegī* pertaining to a family.
خانه *xāne* house.
خبر *xabar* information, news.
خبرگزاری *xabar-gozārī* news agency.

خبر نگار *xabar-negār* newspaper correspondent.
خر *xar* donkey.
خراب *xarāb* } devastation,
خرابی *xarābī* } destruction.
خربزه *xarboze* melon.
خرده *xorde* small piece, bit. *yek xorde* a little.
خرس *xers* bear.
خرطوم *xorṭūm* trunk, proboscis.
خرگوش *xargūš* hare.
خرمن *xarman* stack.
خروج *xorūǰ* going out, egress.
خروس *xorūs* cock.
خریدن *xarīdan* to buy.
خسارت *xasārat* loss, damage.
خشک *xošk* dry. *xošk o xālī* empty.
خشکیدن *xoškīdan* to dry up.
خفقان *xafaqān* palpitation.
خلاص *xalāṣ* } deliverance,
خلاصی *xalāṣī* } liberation.
خلاف *xelāf* contradiction. *bar xelāf-e* contrary to.
خمیر *xamīr* dough.
خنک *xonok* cool.
خواب *xvāb* sleep.
خواباندن *xvābāndan* to put to sleep; to make lie down.
خوابیدن *xvābīdan* to sleep; to lie down.
خواستن *xvāstan* to wish, want.
خواندن *xvāndan* to read.
خوب *xūb* good; well.
خوبی *xūbī* goodness.
خود داری *xod-dārī* restraint. *xod-dārī kardan* to refrain.
خوراک *xorāk* food.
خوردن *xordan* to eat. *be ... xordan* to hit, touch, suit ...
خورزوق *xorzūq* Khorzuq.
خورشید *xoršīd* sun.
خوش *xoš* good, pleasant. *xošaš āmad* he liked it.
خوش اندام *xoš-andām* shapely, symmetrical.
خوشبو *xošbū* pleasant-smelling, fragrant.
خوش پشم *xoš-pašm* having a good coat of fur.
خوشحال *xošḥāl* pleased.
خوش رنگی *xoš-rangī* (state of) having a pretty colour.
خوشمزه *xošmaze* pleasant-tasting, tasty.
خیلی *xei̯lī* very; many, much.

د

داخل *dāxel* entering.
دادن *dādan* to give.
دارائی *dārā'ī* wealth.
داشتن *dāštan* to have.
دان *dān* grain.
دانستن *dānestan* to know (*savoir*).
دانشجو *dānešǰū* student.
دانه *dāne* grain.
دختر *doxtar* daughter; girl.
در *dar* door.
دراز *derāz* long.
در آمدن *dar-āmadan* to come out, appear.
در آوردن *dar-āvordan* to bring out, produce.
در بردن *dar-bordan* to carry off.
درخت *deraxt* tree.
درد *dard* pain. *bedard xordan* to be of use.
درزی *darzī* tailor.
درست *dorost* true, proper; properly.
درشت *dorošt* coarse; large.
درشکه *doroške* carriage.
در گذشتن *dar-gozaštan* to pass away, die.
در گرفتن *dar-gereftan* to break out.
درو *derou̯* (act of) reaping.
دزد *dozd* thief.
دسامبر *desāmbr* December.

دست *dast* hand. *bedast āmadan* to be available. *bedast āvordan* to acquire. *bedast rasīdan* to become available.
دست برد *dast-bord* rapine.
دست گرد *dast-gerd* Dastgerd.
دست نماز *dast-namāz* ablution before prayer.
دسته *daste* group.
دستیاری *dastyārī* complicity, aid.
دشمن *došman* enemy.
دعا *doʿā* prayer *doʿa xvāndan* to pray.
دفاع *defāʿ* defence.
دکان *dokkān* shop.
دل *del* heart.
دلار *dolār* dollar.
دلیرانه *delīrāne* brave, courageous.
دم *dam* breath; edge. *dam-e dar* at the door; to the door.
دم *dom* tail.
دنبال *donbāl* trail. *donbāl-e* (following) after. *donbāl-e ... gaštan* to be looking for ...
دندان *dandān* tooth.
دنیا *donyā* world.
دو *do* two.
دوباره *dobāre* again.
دوختن *dūxtan* to sew.
دور *dour* circumference. *dour-e* around. *dour o bar* environs.
دور *dūr* far. *az dūr* from afar.
دولت *doulat* state, power; government.
دولت آباد *doulat-ābād* Doulatabad.
دوم *dovvom* second.
دویدن *davīdan* to run.
دویست *devīst* two hundred.
ده *deh* village.
دهان *dahān* mouth.
دهستان *dehestān* sub-district.
دهق *dehaq* Dehaq.
دهکده *dehkade* village.
دهلی *dehlī* Delhi.
دهن *dahan* mouth.
دیدن *dīdan* to see; to experience.
دیروز *dīrūz* yesterday.
دیزل *dīzel* Diesel.
دیگر *dīgar* other; any more.
دیوار *dīvār* wall.

ذ

ذرت *zorrat* maize.

ر

راجع *rāǰeʿ* referring. *rāǰeʿ be* with reference to, regarding.
راحت *rāḥat* comfortable; comfortably.
راحتی *rāḥatī* comfort.
رادیو *rādiyo* radio.
راه *rāh* road. *rāh-e āhan* railway *berāh oftādan* to set out.
راه بردار *rāh-bardār* able to find one's way.
رختخواب *raxtexvāb* bed clothes.
رسانیدن *rasānīdan* to cause to arrive; to ripen.
رسد *rasad* share.
رسیدن *rasīdan* to arrive; to ripen.
رشت *rašt* Resht.
رشته *rešte* thread.
رعایا *roʿāyā* peasants. (Pl. of *raʿīyat*.)
رف *raf* upper shelf.
رفتار *raftār* behaviour.
رفتن *raftan* to go.
رفته رفته *rafte-rafte* gradually.
رفیق *rafīq* companion.
رنگ *rang* colour; dye. *rang kardan* to dye.
رنگ رز *rang-raz* dyer.
رنگی *rangī* coloured; dyed.
رنگیدن *rangīdan* to dye.

رو *rū* face. *havā rū besardī raft* the weather began to get cold. *rū-ye* on.
روان *ravān* flowing.
روبراه *rū-berāh* prepared, ready to start.
روپیه *rūpiye* rupee.
روحیه *ruḥīye* mentality, morale.
روز *rūz* day.
روزنامه *rūznāme* newspaper.
روس *rūs* Russian.
روش *raveš* policy.
روشن *roušan* light, bright.
روشنائی *roušanā'ī* light.
روغن *rouγan* oil, fat, ghee.
روم *rūm* Rum (Asia Minor).
روی *rūi* face. *rūi āvordan* to turn (towards).
رویه *ravīye* policy.
رویهم رفته *rūyeham rafte* on an average.
رهسپار *rahsepār* setting out.
ریال *riyāl* rial.
ریختن *rīxtan* to pour, spill; to fall.
ریسیدن *rīsīdan* to spin.
ریشه *rīše* root.

ز

زارع *zāre'* cultivator. *mard-e zāre'* id.
زدن *zadan* to strike, knock; to play (a musical instrument); to rise (the sun). *xodrā bemordan zadan* to pretend to be dead.
زراعت *zerā'at* agriculture.
زرد *zard* yellow.
زرد رنگ *zard-rang* yellow-coloured.
زغال *zoγāl* charcoal.
زمستان *zamestān* winter.
زمستانی *zamestānī* pertaining to the winter.
زمین *zamin* earth, land.
زمینی *zamīnī* pertaining to earth, land.
زن *zan* woman.
زنبور *zanbūr* bee, wasp. *zanbūr-e 'asal* bee.
زندان *zendān* prison.
زندگانی *zendegānī* } life.
زندگی *zendegī* } life.
زود *zūd* early; soon.
زور *zūr* force.
زیاد *ziyād* much.
زیبا *zībā* beautiful.
زیر *zīr* underneath. *zīr-e* under. *zīr o rū kardan* to turn upside down.
زیر دست *zīr-dast* Zirdast.

ژ

ژاپون *žāpon* Japan.
ژنرال *ženerāl* general.

س

ساجی *sāǰī* baked on a grid.
ساختمان *sāxtemān* construction.
ساختن *sāxtan* to make.
سازش *sāzeš* agreement.
ساعت *sā'at* hour.
ساقط *sāqeṭ* falling. *sāqeṭ az hastī* deprived of one's possessions.
سال *sāl* year.
سانتیمتر *sāntīmetr* centimetre.
سایر *sāyer* other.
سبز *sabz* green. *sabz šodan* to sprout.
سپس *sepas* then.
سخت *saxt* hard, strong.
سر *sar* head; end. *sar-e ham kardan* to accumulate.
سرازیر *sarāzīr* sloping. *sarāzīr šodan* to descend.
سراغ *sorāγ* search.
سرباز *sarbāz* soldier.
سر پرستی *sar-parastī* patronage.
سرد *sard* cold.
سردی *sardī* coldness.

سر شیر *sar-šīr* cream.
سر گردان *sar-gardān* wandering.
سر گرم *sar-garm* busy, occupied.
سرما *sarmā* cold, chill. *sarmā xordan* to catch a cold.
سرمایه دار *sarmāye-dār* capitalist.
سعدی *saʿdī* Saʿdi.
سعی *saʿy* endeavour.
سفید *sefīd* white.
سفیر *safīr* envoy, ambassador. *safīr-e kabīr* ambassador.
سکه *sekke* coin.
سگ *sag* dog.
سم *som* hoof.
سنجد *senǰed* service (-tree).
سو *sū* direction. *besū-ye* towards.
سوار *savār* horseman. *savār šodan* to ride.
سواری *savārī* (1) (act of) riding. *savārī dādan* to be used for riding.
سواری *savārī* (2) pertaining to riding. *asb-e savārī* saddle-horse.
سؤال *so'āl* question.
سوختن *sūxtan* to burn. *delaš sūxt* he felt sorry.
سود *sūd* profit, advantage.
سوراخ *sūrāx* hole. *sūrāx kardan* to pierce.
سوسیالیست *sosiyālīst* Socialist.
سوم *sevvom* third(ly).
سوئز *sū'ez* Suez.
سه *se* three.
سی *sī* thirty.
سیاه *siyāh* black.
سیب *sīb* apple.
سیصد *sīṣad* three hundred.
سیل *seil* flood.

ش

شاخ *šāx* horn.
شام *šām* supper.
شاهزاده *šāhzāde* prince.
شایان *šāyān* worthy.
شب *šab* night.
شخص *šaxṣ* person.
شخم *šoxm* (act of) ploughing.
شرط *šarṭ* condition, stipulation. *šarṭ bastan* to make a wager.
شرکت *šerkat* company.
ششصد *šešṣad* six hundred.
شش گوشه *šeš-gūše* hexagonal.
شعر باف *šaʿr-bāf* weaver.
شکار *šekār* hunting, the chase.
شکستن *šekastan* to break; to break off.
شکم *šekam* belly, stomach.
شمع *šamʿ* candle.
شنیدن *šanīdan* to hear.
شوروی *šouravī* Soviet.
شوری *šūrā* council.
شهر *šahr* town.
شهربانی *šahrbānī* police.
شهری *šahrī* pertaining to the town.
شیر *šīr* milk.
شیرین *šīrin* sweet.
شیرینی *šīrīnī* sweetness.
شیطان *šeiṭān* Satan.
شیهه *šīhe* (sound of) neighing. *šīhe kašīdan* to neigh.

ص

صبح *ṣobḥ* morning; in the morning.
صحبت *ṣoḥbat* conversation, talk
صحرا *ṣaḥrā* desert, plain, open country.
صد *ṣad* hundred.
صحرائی *ṣaḥrā'ī* pertaining to the desert, plain, open country.
صدا *ṣedā* voice, sound. *ṣedā zadan* to call, cry.
صراحةً *ṣerāḥatan* explicitly.
صرف *ṣarf* expense. *ṣarf-e naẓar az* apart from. *az ... ṣarf-e naẓar kardan* to dispense with ...

صف *ṣaff* row, line. *ṣaff kašīdan* to draw up in line.
صفا *ṣafā* pleasantness.
صنایع *ṣanāye'* industries. (Pl. of *ṣan'at*.)
صنعت *ṣan'at* art, industry.
صنعتی *ṣan'atī* artistic, industrial.
صورت *ṣūrat* shape, form; case. *dar ṣūratīke* in case. *ṣūrat gereftan* to be realized.

ض

ضخیم *ẓaxīm* bulky.
ضمن *ẓemn* middle. *dar ẓemn-e* in the course of. *ẓemn-e* id.
ضمناً *ẓemnan* meanwhile; incidentally.

ط

طاقچه *ṭāqče* shelf.
طبق *ṭebq* conformity. *ṭebq-e* in accordance with.
طرف *ṭaraf* side. *az ṭaraf-e* on behalf of; from, by. *az ṭaraf-e dīgar* on the other hand.
طرفین *ṭarafein* the two sides.
طلا *ṭelā* gold.
طول *ṭūl* length. *ṭūl kašīdan* to last.

ظ

ظرف *ẓarf* vessel, dish; space.

ع

عبارت *'ebārat* phrase, expression. *'ebārat būdan az* to consist of.
عبور *'obūr* crossing, passage.
عجالةً *'ejālatan* for the time being.
عرض *'arẓ* width.
عرعر *'ar'ar* (sound of) braying.
عزیمت *'azīmat* setting out; undertaking, enterprise.
عسل *'asal* honey.
عقل *'aql* reason; wisdom.
علف *'alaf* grass.
عمارت *'emārat* building.
عمامه *'ammāme* turban.
عمل *'amal* action. *be'amal āvordan* to carry out; to produce. *be'amal āmadan* to be produced.
عملی *'amalī* practicable. *'amalī kardan* to carry out, enforce.
عمومی *'omūmī* general, public.
عوارض *'avāreẓ* dues.

غ

غالب *γāleb* greater part, most.
غرامات *γarāmāt* reparations.
غربیل *γarbīl* riddle, coarse sieve.
غلتک *γaltak* roller, cylinder.
غلغله *γolγole* uproar, tumult. *γolγole-ye rūm* a great uproar.
غوزه *γūze* cotton-pod.
غیر *γeir-e* other than, non-.

ف

فائده *fā'ede* use, advantiage.
فدا *fedā* sacrifice.
فرار *ferār* flight, escape.
فراری *ferārī* fugitive.
فراغت *farāγat* ease, quiet.
فرانسوی *farānsavī* French.
فرانسه *farānse* France; French.
فراهم *farāham* collected together. *farāham kardan* to provide, bring about.

فرق *farq* difference.
فرمودن *farmūdan* to command; to say.
فرو بردن *forū-bordan* to thrust.
فروختن *forūxtan* to sell.
فرود آوردن *forūd-āvordan* to bring down; to bow.
فریاد *faryād* cry, shout. *faryād zadan* to cry out.
فصل *faṣl* season.
فعلاً *feʿlan* at present.
فعلی *feʿlī* present.
فقط *faqaṭ* only.
فقیر *faqīr* poor.
فکر *fekr* thought, idea.
فلسطین *falasṭin* Palestine.
فوق *fouq* above.
فهمیدن *fahmīdan* to understand.
فیل *fīl* elephant.
فیلسوف *feilasūf* philosopher.

ق

قارقار *qārqār* (sound of) croaking, cawing.
قبا *qabā* cloak.
قبول *qabūl* acceptance. *qabūl dāštan* to accept.
قدقد *qodqod* (sound of) clucking.
قدیمی *qadīmī* ancient, old.
قراء *qorāʾ* villages. (Pl. of *qarye*.)
قرار *qarār* rest; arrangement. *beqarār-e* according to. *qarār gozāštan* to arrange.
قرار داد *qarār-dād* agreement.
قریب *qarīb* near. *qarīb-e* nearly, almost.
قریه *qarye* village.
قسم *qesm* kind, sort.
قشنگ *qašang* pretty, beautiful.
قصبه *qaṣabe* small town.
قصه *qeṣṣe* story, tale.
قله *qolle* top, summit.
قنات *qanāt* subterranean water-channel.
قنوات *qanavāt* (Pl. of *qanāt*).
قوانین *qavānin* laws. (Pl. of *qānūn*.)
قوت *qūt* food.
قوت *qovvat* strength.
قوچ *qūč* ram.
قیمت *qeimat* value.

ک

کار *kār* work, affair.
کارخانه *kārxāne* factory, workshop.
کارگر *kārgar* worker.
کارمل *kārmel* Carmel.
کاشتن *kāštan* to sow.
کافی *kāfī* sufficient.
کاملاً *kāmelan* perfectly.
کامیون *kāmiyon* lorry.
کانال *kānāl* canal.
کاه *kāh* straw.
کبیر *kabīr* great.
کر *kar* deaf.
کردن *kardan* to make, do.
کرم *kerm* worm.
کروسین *kerosin* kerosene.
کره *kare* butter.
کره *korre* foal.
کشاورز *kešāvarz* cultivator.
کشت *kešt* (sown) field.
کشتن *keštan* to sow.
کشته *kešte* seed.
کشتی *kaštī* ship.
کشور *kešvar* land, country.
کشیدن *kašīdan* to draw, pull.
کلاغ *kalāɣ* crow.
کلی *kollī* general, universal. *bekollī* entirely.
کلیه *kollīye* totality, all.
کم *kam* few, little. *kamtar* less, less often.
کماج *komāǰ* thick, flat, round loaf.
کمپانی *kompānī* company.
کمک *komak* help.

کم‌کم *kam-kam* little by little, gradually.
کمکی *komakī* auxiliary.
کنج *konǰ* corner.
کندن *kandan* to pluck.
کنفرانس *konferāns* conference.
کو *kū* where is, are ?
کوبیدن *kūbīdan* to beat, pound; to thresh.
کوتاه *kūtāh* short.
کوچک *kūčak* little, small.
کوچیک *kūčik* coll. form of *kūčak*.
کوشش *kūšeš* endeavour.
کوه *kūh* mountain.
کوهستان *kūhestān* mountainous country.
کیفر *keịfar* punishment.
کیلومتر *kīlometr* kilometre.
کیونک *kiyūnak* Kiyunak.

گ

گاری *gārī* cart.
گاو *gāv* ox, cow. *gāv-e māde* cow. *gāv-e nar* bull.
گاو آهن *gāv-āhan* ploughshare.
گاه *gāh* time. *gāhī* sometimes.
گذاشتن *gozāštan* to let, allow; to put, place.
گذشتن *gozaštan* to pass.
گذشته *gozašte* past. *gozašte az* apart from.
گرد آمدن *gerd-āmadan* to gather together.
گرد آوردن *gerd-āvordan* to accumulate.
گردن *gardan* neck.
گرده *gorde* back (of an animal).
گردیدن *gardīdan* to become.
گرفتن *gereftan* to take, sieze.
گرم *garm* warm, hot. *saraš-garm ast* he is busy.
گرما *garmā* } warmth, heat.
گرمی *garmī* }
گریختن *gorīxtan* to flee.
گز *gaz* Gaz.
گزارش *gozāreš* report. *gozāreš-dādan* to report.
گشتن *gaštan* to become.
گفتن *goftan* to say, to call.
گل *gol* flower.
گلابی *golābī* pear.
گلدسته *goldaste* bouquet; minaret.
گمان *gamān* supposition.
گمرکی *gomrokī* pertaining to frontier customs.
گنجشک *gonǰešk* sparrow.
گندم *gandom* wheat.
گوسفند *gūsfand* sheep.
گوش *gūš* ear. *gūš-e šeịṭān kar* may Satan's ear be deaf, i.e. may he not disturb this pleasure!
گوشه *gūše* corner.
گویا *gūyā* perhaps.
گیاه *giyāh* plant, herb.

ل

لا *lā* fold. *lā-ye* inside, amongst.
لاک پشت *lāk-pošt* tortoise.
لانه *lāne* nest.
لب *lab* lip; edge. *lab-e* at the edge of.
لباس *lebās* clothing, garment.
لحاظ *leḥāẓ* respect, point of view. *az leḥāẓ-e* with respect to.
لذا *leẕā* therefore.
لذت *lazzat* pleasure.
لطیف *laṭīf* thin, delicate.
لعاب *lo‘āb* saliva.
لندن *landan* London.
لواش *lavāš* thin, flat (bread).

م

مادر *mādar* mother.
ماده *māde* female.
ماست *māst* yoghourt.
ماشین *māšin* machine.

ماک ارتور *māk artūr* MacArthur.
مال *māl* property.
ماليخوليا *mālīxūliyā* madness.
ماله *māle* harrow. *māle kašīdan* to harrow.
ماندن *māndan* to remain.
مانندِ *mānand-e* like.
مایه *māye* yeast. *māye zadan* to leaven.
مبادله *mobādele* exchange.
مبلغ *mablaγ* sum, amount.
متخصص *motaxaṣṣeṣ* specialist.
متضمن *motaẓammen* containing.
متفق *mottafeq* allied, united.
متمول *motamavvel* rich.
متوجه *motavaǰǰeh* facing, directed towards; attentive.
متوقف *motavaqqef* halted, suspended.
مجاور *moǰāver* neighbouring.
مجروح *maǰrūḥ* wounded.
مجلس *maǰles* assembly. *maǰles-e šūrā-ye mellī* National Consultative Assembly.
محاصره *moḥāṣere* siege, blockade.
محرک *moḥarrek* instigator.
محسوب *maḥsūb* reckoned.
محصولات *maḥṣūlāt* products.
محفوظ *maḥfūẓ* protected.
محکم *moḥkam* firm, strong, solid.
محل *maḥall* place.
مدت *moddat* while, space of time.
مذاکره *mozākere* discussion.
مراجعه *morāǰe'e* reference.
مراقب *morāqeb* watching, observing.
مربوط *marbūṭ* connected.
مرتبه *martabe* degree; time. *yek martabe* once; all at once.
مرد *mard* man.
مردم *mardom* people.
مردن *mordan* to die.
مرده *morde* dead.
مرز *marz* frontier, boundary.
مرغ *morγ* bird; fowl, hen.
مرور *morūr* passage.
مزارع *mazāre'* fields. (Pl. of *mazra'e*.)
مزبور *mazbūr* aforesaid.
مزد *mozd* wages.
مستثنی *mostaṣnā* excepted.
مستر *mester* Mr.
مستلزم *mostalzem* necessitating, requiring.
مسکون *maskūn* habitable.
مسلح *mosallaḥ* armed.
مسلط *mosalleṭ* dominating.
مسلمان *mosalmān* Moslem.
مشروع *mašrū'* legal.
مشغول *mašγūl* occupied.
مصر *meṣr* Egypt.
مطالبه *moṭālebe* claim, demand.
معاش *ma'āš* livelihood.
معاون *mo'āven* assistant; under-secretary.
معروف *ma'rūf* well-known.
معظم *mo'ẓam* great.
مغز *maγz* marrow; kernel.
مفقودالاثر *mafqūdo'laṣar* lost without trace.
مقابل *moqābel* opposite. *dar moqābel-e* opposite(to), vis-à-vis.
مقاله *maqāle* article.
مقررات *moqarrarāt* regulations.
مکنت *meknat* wealth.
مکنیل *maknīl* McNeil.
مکیدن *mekīdan* to suck.
ملا *mollā* mulla.
ملامت *malāmat* reproach.
ملت *mellat* nation.
ملحق *molhaq* joined.
ملل *melal* nations. (Pl. of *mellat*.)
ملی *mellī* national. *mellī kardan* to nationalize.
مليون *melyūn* million.
ممکن *momken* possible.
منچستر *manchester* Manchester.

منچستر گاردیان *manchester gārdiyān* Manchester Guardian.
منزل *manzel* stage; dwelling, house. *bemanzel rasīdan* to reach one's destination.
منظور *manẕūr* aim, object.
منعقد *mon'aqed* concluded.
منعقده *mon'aqede* fem. of *mon'aqed*.
منقول *manqūl* movable. *γeịr-e manqūl* immovable.
منهدم *monhadem* destroyed.
مو *mū* hair.
مواد *mavādd* articles. (Pl. of *mādde.*)
موافقت *movāfeqat* agreement.
موجب *mūǰab* consequence, result. *bemūǰab-e* in accordance with.
مور *mūr* } ant.
مورچه *mūrče* } ant.
مورد *moured* instance, case. *moured-e* object of. *moured-e niyāz* needed.
مور مور *mūr-mūr* pins and needles.
موضع *mouze'* position.
موضوع *mouzū'* subject, question.
موظف *movaẕẕaf* charged, bound.
موفق *movaffaq* successful.
موقع *mouqe'* time.
موم *mūm* wax.
مهاجر *mohāǰer* emigrant.
مهاجرت *mohāǰerat* emigration.
مهم *mohemm* important; chief, main.
مهیب *mohīb* dreadful, terrible.
میان *miyān* middle. *miyān-e* among. *miyān-e rāh* en route.
میش *mīš* ewe.
میکادو *mīkādo* Mikado.
میلیارد *mīliyārd* billion.
میلیون *mīlyūn* million.
میوه *mīve* fruit.

ن

نا امید *nā-omīd* desperate.
نابودی *nābūdī* annihilation.
ناچیز *nāčīz* insignificant.
نازک *nāzok* thin, slender; delicate.
نا گوار *nā-govār* unpalatable; unpleasant.
نامه *nāme* letter.
نان *nān* bread.
نتیجه *natīǰe* result. *dar natīǰe-ye* as a result of.
نجات *naǰāt* salvation.
نجیب *naǰīb* noble.
نخ *nax* (cotton) yarn.
نخ تاب *nax-tāb* spinner.
نخست *noxost* first. *noxost vazīr* prime minister.
نر *nar* male.
نرم *narm* soft.
نزدیک *nazdīk* near. *nazdīk ast berasad* he is about to arrive.
نشاسته *nešāste* starch.
نشان *nešān* sign, mark. *nešān dādan* to show.
نشستن *nešastan* to sit.
نصیحت *naṣīḥat* advice.
نطق *noṭq* speech.
نظامی *neẕāmī* military.
نظر *naẕar* view. *naẕar be-inke* in view of the fact that. *dar naẕar gereftan* to take into consideration.
نفت *naft* petroleum.
نفر *nafar* individual, person.
نفس *nafas* breath. *nafas kašīdan* to breathe
نقد *naqd* cash. *pūl-e naqd* ready money.
نقل *naql* transport.
نقره *noqre* silver.
نقشه *naqše* plan.
نکته *nokte* point.
نگاه *negāh* look, glance.

نگاهداشتن *negāhdāštan* to keep.
نگهبان *negahbān* guard.
نگهداشتن *negahdāštan* to keep.
نماز *namāz* prayer.
نمودن *namūdan* to show.
نواحی *navāḥī* districts. (Pl. of *nāḥiye.*)
نود *navad* ninety.
نوشتن *neveštan* to write.
نوع *nou̯ʿ* kind, sort.
نوک *nūk* beak.
نه *noh* nine.
نیاز *niyāz* need.
نیت *nīyat* intention, purpose.
نیرو *nīrū* strength, force.
نیز *nīz* also.
نیم *nīm* half.
نیمه شب *nīme-šab* midnight.

و

وارد *vāred* arriving; sustained. *vāred kardan* to import.
وارده *vārede* fem. of *vāred.*
واقع *vāqeʿ* lying, situated.
واقعه *vāqeʿe* event, happening.
واق واق *vāq-vāq* (sound of) barking.
وا کردن *vā-kardan* to open.
وجود *vou̯ǰūd* existence, presence.
وحدت *vaḥdat* unity, unification.
وخامت *vaxāmat* badness, dangerousness.
ور داشتن *var-dāštan* to pick up.
وزارت *vezārat* ministry.
وزیدن *vazīdan* to blow.
وزیر *vazīr* minister.
وسایل *vasāyel* means. (Pl. of *vasīle.*)
وسیله *vasīle* means, medium. *bevasīle-ye* by means of.
وطن *vaṭan* native land.
وقایع *vaqāyeʿ* incidents. (Pl. of *vāqeʿe.*)
وقت *vaqt* time. *ān vaqt* then. *vaqtī ke.* when
ویران *vīrān* ruined, desolate.

ه

هجوم *hoǰūm* assault.
هدف *hadaf* target, goal, object.
هر *har* every. *har kas* everyone. *har gāh* whenever, if; *har če* whatever.
هرزه *harze* dissolute. *ʿalaf-e harze* weed.
هزار *hazār* thousand.
هستی *hastī* existence; wealth, property.
هلاکت *halākat* destruction.
هم *ham* (1) also.
هم *ham* (2) one another. *beham* together.
همان *hamān* that very, the same.
همچنین *hamčonin* likewise.
همسایه *hamsāye* neighbour.
همگی *hamegī* totality, all.
هموار *hamvār* level.
همه *hame* all. *hame ǰā* everywhere. *bā in hame* nevertheless.
همین *hamin* this very, the same. *hamin ke* as soon as.
هندوستان *hendūstān* India.
هندی *hendī* Indian, Hindu.
هنگام *hangām* time. *hangāmī ke* when.
هنوز *hanūz* yet, still.
هو *hou̯* hoot. *yek hou̯* all of a sudden.
هوا *havā* air; weather.
هوا پیما *havā-pei̯mā* aeroplane.
هیزم *hīzom* wood, firewood.

ی

یابو *yābū* pack-horse.

یاد *yād* memory. *yād oftādan* to be remembered, come to mind.

یافتن *yāftan* to find.

یال *yāl* mane.

یالّا *yāllā* get up! (Coll. form of *yā allāh.*)

یخ *yax* ice. *yax kardan* to be freezing.

یعنی *ya'nī* i.e.

یک *yak* one, a. *yakī būd yaki nabūd* once upon a time.

یکساله *yaksāle* (sufficient) for one year.

یکسان *yaksān* equal. *be yaksān* equally.

ین *yen* yen.

یواشکی *yavāšakī* slowly.

یونان *yūnān* Greece.

یهودی *yahūdī* Jew.